The FA

LEARNING

The Official FA Guide to
Basic Team Coaching

Les Reed
The Football Association's Acting Technical Director

Hodder & Stoughton

A MEMBER OF THE HODDER HEADLINE GROUP

For order enquiries: please contact Bookpoint Ltd, 130 Milton Park, Abingdon, Oxon
OX14 4SB. Telephone: +44 (0) 1235 827720. Fax: +44 (0) 1235 400454. Lines are open
from 09.00–18.00, Monday to Saturday with a 24-hour message answering service.
Details about our titles and how to order are available at www.madaboutbooks.com

British Library Cataloguing in Publication Data:
a catalogue record for this title is available from the British Library.

ISBN 0 340 816007

First Published 2004
Impression number   10 9 8 7 6 5 4 3
Year   2007 2006 2005 2004

Copyright © 2004 FA Learning Ltd

Managing Editor: Jonathan Wilson, FA Learning

Typeset by Servis Filmsetting Ltd, Manchester.
Printed in Great Britain for Hodder Arnold, a division of Hodder Headline Ltd,
338 Euston Road, London NW1 3BH by Cox & Wyman, Reading, Berkshire.

Hodder Headline's policy is to use papers that are natural, renewable and recyclable
products and made from wood grown in sustainable forests. The logging and
manufacturing processes are expected to conform to the environmental regulations of the
country of origin.

Contents

LEARNING

Sven-Goran Eriksson

Philosophy of the guides

The aim of these **Official FA Guides** is to reach the millions of people who participate in football or who are involved in the game in other ways – at any level.

Each book aims to increase your awareness and understanding of association football and in this understanding to enhance, increase, improve and extend your involvement in the world's greatest game.

These books are designed to be interactive and encourage you to apply what you read and to help you to translate this knowledge into practical skills and ability. Specific features occur throughout this book to assist this process:

■ Tasks will appear in this form and will make you think about what you have just learned and how you will apply it in a practical way.

Best Practice The Best Practice feature will give you an example of a good or ideal way of doing things – this could be on or off the pitch.

Quote | 'Quotes throughout will pass on useful knowledge or insight or encourage you to consider a certain aspect of your skills or responsibilities.'

Statistic

The statistics included will often surprise and will certainly increase your knowledge of the game.

Summary

- **The summaries at the end of each chapter will recap on its contents and help you to consolidate your knowledge and understanding.**

You can read this guide in any way you choose and prefer to do so – at home, on the pitch, in its entirety, or to dip in for particular advice. Whatever way you use it, we hope it increases your ability, your knowledge, your involvement, and most importantly your enjoyment and passion to **be a part of the game**.

Introduction

This book is an introduction to football team coaching for the individual who aspires to be, or is already, the coach of a football team. It is assumed that the team is 11-a-side with players who are at least 13 years of age, and who can attempt the full range of techniques of the game. Players younger than 13 may attempt the practices outlined but it is unlikely they will possess the full range of techniques.

For real improvement, the reader should practise coaching as much as possible, evaluate their own coaching sessions, watch good coaches work and take advantage of the range of Football Association (The FA) courses available (**www.TheFA.com**/FALearning).

The book should be seen as a guide for the aspiring coach or existing coach to dip into whenever the occasion merits a single reference. Please do not look upon the book as a manual – it is not intended to provide the answer to every problem – if there could be such a publication. Each chapter outlines some of the aspects of coaching a team but do not dwell upon the coaching points of technique because the team coach is unlikely to have the time to be able to coach players individually. The coach should refer to other publications that deal with individual techniques.

At all times it is assumed that the coach will insist upon strict adherence to 'Laws of the Game'. These laws ensure that practices are conducted in a fair and safe environment and that skilful attacking is encouraged as much as the individual deploying skilful defending to combat such innovation and guile.

It is important that the facilities and equipment used are safe and do not pose a risk to the players, and that the players use the appropriate footwear and shin guards in practices involving opponents. The FA's guidelines for goalpost safety should be adhered to (see **www.TheFA.com**/TheFA/FAcampaigns). Where full-size goals are recommended, these should be of the required dimensions. For practices where full-size goals are not available, goals should be marked with cones placed to mark the required width.

The material for this guide has been collated from many sources: Liverpool John Moores University; Dr Dave Houlston of Coachwise Ltd; the experience of our national coaches with teams; *Insight* – the journal of The FA Coaches Association; the official publications of The FA written by the National Coaches and Directors of Coaching including Walter Winterbottom, Allen Wade, Charles Hughes, Bobby Robson and Howard Wilkinson.

In particular I would like to acknowledge the assistance provided by my colleague, Robin Russell, the Project Director of FA Learning, in editing this guide.

The FA is pleased to acknowledge all their contributions to this guide.

Les Reed
Acting Technical Director
April 2004

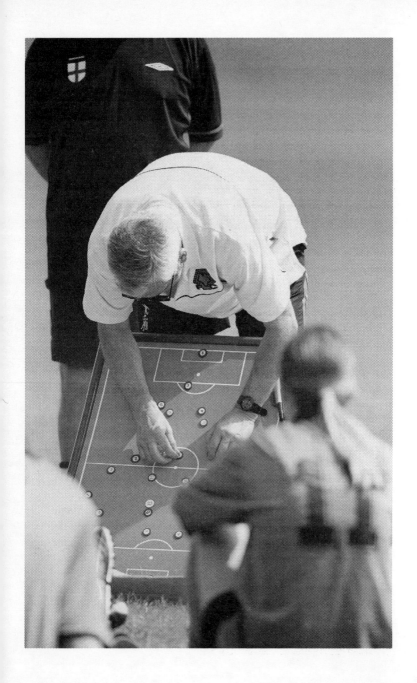

The FA
LEARNING

Chapter 1

Coaching: ethics and skills

THIS CHAPTER WILL:

- Help you to understand the codes of behaviour applicable to the role of an Association Football coach.
- Show you how to identify and challenge inappropriate ethical behaviour and conduct displayed by yourself and other coaches.
- Give you an understanding of the expectations that the game of football places on coaches' behaviour and conduct.
- Help you to communicate and support the expectations of The Football Association Code of Conduct to players and others involved in sport.
- Demonstrate a range of coaching methods and their application.
- Show you how to communicate positively, ethically and effectively with players and others.
- Outline how to encourage positive and effective communication between football players and others.
- Explain how to resolve conflict between players, and between players and others.

Ethics, fair play and codes of behaviour

What are coaching principles?

All football coaches have beliefs and opinions about what coaching is and how coaches can help players. Some might believe that players, especially young players, should not be coached but should be allowed to develop by themselves; other coaches might believe players should be nurtured carefully from an early age to avoid the development of bad habits and particular weaknesses.

Your view is based on how you learned to play football, on your present knowledge and on your future expectations. Your coaching is affected by your beliefs, attitudes and motives. These factors will influence your reasons for wanting to coach and provide the personal, moral and ethical principles that guide your coaching.

Will you, for example, condone cheating, allow swearing, or punish players for a poor performance? Or will you promote fair play and honesty, and reward effort? Are you more interested in producing winning teams than improving players? You might hold specific views about the relative value of competition and winning. It would be in the best interests of your players to balance the importance of winning with other objectives, for example, development or enjoyment.

These are significant ingredients in the game of football, but possibly not as significant for young players as the development of sound technique. If you are unsure about your beliefs, you need to define them because finding out about yourself helps you to outline your coaching principles.

Coaching principles and football

You should share your coaching principles with players, parents, club members and fellow coaches so that they can clearly understand your beliefs and motives. For instance, if a young player comes to you seeking general improvement but is groomed by you to play wingback as part of your strategy for a winning team, the chances are you will frustrate and demotivate this player and probably upset the parents.

This example highlights the coaching principle of helping players to meet their own ambitions as well as embracing positive interpersonal behaviours such as self-control, honesty, fairness, equality and dignity. For instance, do you encourage your players to accept refereeing decisions even though your opponents appear intent on disagreeing with them? How do you react when one of your own players is arguing with an official or a teammate, or towards a parent who is negatively criticizing his own child from the touchline?

Your answers to such questions reflect your coaching principles, and you should be prepared to discuss this with other coaches. What you consider to be unacceptable principles might be acceptable to other coaches, or vice versa.

Principles of successful coaching

The principles you uphold will be evident in your behaviour towards others, and in how you expect people to behave towards you. Principles of successful coaching might include:

- **Respecting the needs of individuals and treating all players fairly.**
- **Developing independence by encouraging players and other coaches to accept responsibility for their own behaviour.**
- **The development of individuals as people as well as football players.**
- **The development of mutual trust, respect and commitment.**
- **Positive acknowledgement of progress and achievement.**
- **Communication with players, coaches, parents and other helpers or support agencies (e.g. schools, medical practitioners).**

- Promoting fair play within the Laws of the Game and respecting the dignity of opponents and officials.
- Accepting responsibility for the conduct of players and encouraging positive social and moral behaviours.
- Maintaining confidentiality of information when appropriate to do so.
- Displaying high personal standards of behaviour, dress and communication.
- Ensuring as far as possible the safety and health of players.
- Developing personal competence as a coach.

Based on The FA Sport & Recreation Values Statement for Coaching, Teaching and Instructing, 2000.

Quote | 'The most effective way to develop and improve your coaching skills is to enrol upon an FA Coaching course (**www.TheFA.com**/FALearning) and take as much opportunity to practise your skills as possible.'

The coach's role and responsibility

To gain the respect of players and take reasonable care of them, football coaches need to prepare and organize themselves thoroughly in order to organize other people effectively and safely.

Your role as a football coach goes beyond that of a skilled and knowledgeable technician who is seeking to help players learn and improve. At times throughout your coaching career, you might be called upon to act as a fitness trainer, a social worker, a motivator, a disciplinarian, a friend, a journalist, a mentor, a manager and an administrator as well as many other roles.

For some of these roles, it is important to know where to seek more expert support for yourself and your players; perhaps when evidence of physical abuse is disclosed to you or where a player might be experiencing financial hardship. You will learn through experience how to handle other roles and the most important step in coping with the various parts of the job is to get to know your players.

Coaches are usually held in high esteem by young players and are important role models for children. With such status comes responsibility. The Football Association Coaches Association (FACA) Code of Conduct declares that football coaches must display high personal standards of appearance, behaviour and organization. Most importantly, coaches should accept responsibility for the conduct of their players and encourage positive and non-discriminatory behaviours. Does your club have a Code of Conduct and an equal opportunities policy?

The qualities of a successful coach

Regardless of whether you are naturally lively and enthusiastic or quiet and shy, there are particular personal qualities required by all coaches for them to be effective. These qualities need to be harnessed with coaching skills so that you can help the individuals you coach to achieve their potential and enjoy football.

The qualities of a good coach might include enthusiasm, patience, open-mindedness, fairness, knowledge of the sport, a desire to learn and a willingness to help other people improve. Without these positive personal qualities, the most skilled technical coach might not be able to help people learn effectively.

| Quote | 'Winning isn't everything. Wanting to win is.' (Vince Lombardi, former American football coach) |

Sir Bobby Robson

The Football Association Code of Conduct

Code of Conduct
Football is the world's most popular game. All those involved with the game at every level, whether as a player, match official, coach, owner or administrator, have a responsibility, above and beyond compliance with the law, to act according to the highest standards of integrity, and to ensure that the reputation of the game is, and remains, high. This code applies to all those involved in football under the auspices of The Football Association.

Community
Football, at all levels, is a vital part of a community. Football will take into account community feeling when making decisions.

Equality
Football is opposed to discrimination of any form and will promote measures to prevent it, in whatever form, from being expressed.

Participants
Football recognizes the sense of ownership felt by those who participate at all levels of the game. This includes those who play, those who coach or help in any way, and those who officiate as well as administrators and supporters. Football is committed to appropriate consultation.

Young people
Football acknowledges that public confidence demands the highest standards of financial and administrative behaviour within the game, and will not tolerate corruption or improper practices.

Trust and respect
Football will uphold a relationship of trust and respect between all involved in the game, whether they are individuals, clubs or other organizations.

Violence
Football rejects the use of violence of any nature, by anyone involved in the game.

Fairness
Football is committed to fairness in its dealings with all involved in the game.

Integrity and fair play
Football is committed to the principle of playing to win consistent with fair play.

By order of The FA Council, November 1998

Code of Conduct for coaches

Coaches are key to the establishment of ethics in football. Their concept of ethics and their attitude directly affects the behaviour of players under their supervision. Coaches are, therefore, expected to pay particular care to the moral aspect of their conduct.

Coaches have to be aware that almost all of their everyday decisions and choices of actions, and strategic targets have ethical implications.

It is natural that winning constitutes a basic concern for coaches. This code is not intended to conflict with that. However, the code calls for coaches to disassociate themselves from a 'win-at-all-costs' attitude.

Increased responsibility is requested from coaches involved in coaching young people. The health, safety, welfare and moral education of young people are a first priority, before the achievement or the reputation of the club, school, coach or parent.

Set out below is The FA and Coaches Association (FACA) Codes of Conduct which reflect the standards expressed by sports coach UK (a coaching organization that provides a UK based sports coach education programme), and forms the benchmark for all involved in coaching.

FACA Code of Conduct

- Coaches must respect the rights, dignity and worth of each and every person and treat each equally within the context of the sport.
- Coaches must place the well-being and safety of each player above all other considerations, including the development of performance.
- Coaches must adhere to all guidelines laid down by FACA and the Rules of The Football Association.
- Coaches must develop an appropriate working relationship with each player based on mutual trust and respect.
- Coaches must encourage and guide players to accept responsibility for their own behaviour and performance.

- Coaches must ensure that the activities they direct or advocate are appropriate for the age, maturity, experience and ability of players.
- Coaches should, at the outset, clarify with the players (and where appropriate, parents), exactly what is expected of them and also what they are entitled to expect from their coach.
- Coaches must co-operate fully with other specialists (e.g. other coaches, officials, sports scientists, doctors and physiotherapists) in the best interests of the player.
- Coaches must always promote the positive aspects of the sport (e.g. fair play) and never condone violations of the Laws of the Game, behaviour contrary to the spirit of the Laws of the Game or relevant rules and regulations of the use of prohibited substances or techniques.
- Coaches must consistently display high standards of behaviour and appearance.
- Coaches must not use or tolerate inappropriate language.

Any breach of any provision(s) of this Code of Conduct by a member of The FA Coaches Association shall constitute a breach of the Rules of The Football Association pursuant to Rule 26(a)(x) and shall be dealt with under the procedures as set out in the Rules of The Football Association.

The Football Association and The FA Coaches Association wish to acknowledge the valuable contribution of sports coach UK in creating this Code of Conduct.

Promoting fair play

Very often the personal beliefs and expectations that underpin your coaching are placed under increasing pressure by the interpretation of the Laws of the Game by players, other coaches and officials. Some believe that, due to the rewards on offer, the higher the level of performance, the greater the ethical distance between players and the Laws of the Game.

It is particularly important for coaches of young players to reinforce the importance of the Laws of the Game because they are in place to ensure fairness and justice for all participants. The laws enable the game to be played and any player who deliberately sets out to infringe the laws destroys the essence of the game.

The worst games you have been involved in or remember were the ones in which the laws were broken most frequently or most seriously. They were probably the games least enjoyed by players, spectators, coaches and officials. Very often, post-match analysis reveals distinct differences in people's opinions of what happened and the intentions behind certain behaviours. Was the foul tackle deliberate or accidental? Was the tackler reckless or clumsy?

In addition to the Laws of the Game which should support a minimum standard of behaviour amongst participants, coaches should be responsible for promoting positive forms of personal conduct. For example, players should be encouraged to support teammates, and avoid arguing with officials or spectators.

The FACA Code of Conduct provides guidelines on how coaches can promote fairness and equality in football. Read through the code and reflect on how it relates to your involvement in football. You might also consider how parents and spectators could be included in the code, and how it might be implemented at your club. The FA Code of Conduct is broader and should be promoted by you and your club.

■   Define a simple Code of Conduct involving three do's and three don'ts for the players and officials of your club.

The skills of coaching

Football coaches come from a variety of backgrounds and bring with them their own beliefs, expectations and personal qualities. However, it is possible to identify the common knowledge and skills that underpin effective coaching. These include:

- Teaching players how and when to use techniques and skills in football.
- Communicating with players, parents, other coaches and agencies.
- Asking appropriate questions, providing explanations, using demonstrations, listening and observing what players do.
- Leading and motivating players.
- Planning and preparing sessions to meet players' needs and ensure safety.
- Delivering and controlling coaching sessions to ensure safe practice.
- Analysing performances and guiding relevant progress.
- Organizational and administrative skills (e.g. booking facilities, arranging transport, completing registration forms).

███ List as many different roles that football coaches fulfil as you can. Are there some roles that are more important than others? List your top five. Describe the skills and qualities of a coach.

Quote | 'What I hear I forget.
| What I see I remember.
| What I do, I know.' (Chinese proverb)

Introduction to coaching methods

The purpose of coaching, and the methods employed by coaches, is to help people learn and improve techniques and skills so that they can perform more successfully and effectively. Defining some of these terms and methods might help your communication with players and other coaches.

What is meant by skill and technique?

The term 'skill' whether applied to coaching or playing, refers to an ability to select and implement an appropriate and effective response from a range of possibilities. In other words, a skilled player knows what to do, and when and where to do it. This is different from 'technique', which is a term used to describe a basic action or movement (that is, how to do it).

Techniques form the building blocks on which skills are developed, so that players who have developed the technical ability to produce a particular turn or dribble can employ that technique in the right place at the right time.

What is the difference between learning and performance?

Watching your favourite football team play is like going to the theatre or cinema because you are watching a performance. Such performances are used to assess how teams' and players' performances compare to that of previous occasions. However, learning is a relatively permanent change in behaviour and usually a result of much corrective practice. You should not presume that a technique or skill is learned if it is performed successfully on one occasion.

As coaches, you are looking to help players learn and you use their performances to monitor the effectiveness of this learning. But remember, variation in performance might not be due to lack of skill or technique, it can be affected by other factors such as fatigue, boredom, illness or injury. You need to observe consistent changes in a player's performance of techniques and skills to be sure that learning has taken place.

Whole and part methods

There are two basic methods used to develop techniques and skills. First, they can be undertaken by learning the whole technique or sequence of movements, or second, by breaking the movement or sequence into parts and learning each constituent part. In football coaching it is beneficial for the whole and part methods to be used in combination.

The most effective ways of combining whole and part methods are:

- **Shaping.**
- **Chaining.**
- **Whole-part-whole.**

Each method has strengths and weaknesses, and you should be aware of which method to use in appropriate situations. For instance, techniques are best developed using shaping and chaining, but these approaches can be long-winded and tedious. The whole-part-whole approach promotes more opportunity to test decision making in challenging game-related situations, but might not promote the development of sound techniques.

Shaping

All players, including children, find big movements easier to learn than small, accurate movements. Running is simpler than hopping; passing the ball with the inside of the foot is easier to develop than a drag-back turn. Shaping makes learning a technique more straightforward by leaving out some of the parts to begin with and adding them later. When developing a new technique, coaches need to accept a rough version and shape it gradually into the refined model.

Quote | 'Everyone has the will to win but few have the will to prepare to win.' (Bobby Knight, US basketball coach)

Best Practice Roy Hodgson, the former Blackburn Rovers, Inter Milan and Swiss International Team Manager, summed up his ten factors of developing effective team work:

1 Be positive.
2 Show respect.
3 Have principles, beliefs and a philosophy.
4 Be honest.
5 Be loyal.
6 Be personal.
7 Develop a sense of perspective.
8 Communicate and inform.
9 Accept responsibility.
10 Be humble.

(*Insight*, Issue 2, Volume 2, winter 1998)

Shaping

Shaping might be a useful method to use when helping players to learn the basic long passing action (i.e. using the instep, not the inside of the foot). The movements required to produce the long passing action are difficult to break down into small parts.

At first, the player should be encouraged to make contact with the correct part of the foot (e.g. instep) and kick through the mid-line of the ball. Once this form of contact is regular, the placement of the non-kicking foot could be refined to help in directing the pass. Subsequently, the head, upper body and arm positions can be modified (i.e. they are refined rather than added).

When using shaping to gradually refine a technique, rough forms of the movements are an acceptable basis for progression. Coaches often use links to other movements to guide learners towards an acceptable version. For example, players are often encouraged to 'point to the target' when refining the body position in the long passing technique.

Expert players who wish to modify an existing technique might use it as the basis for shaping the new one.

Shaping can also be applied to decision making and tactical aspects of football. The gradual refinement of players' movements in set pieces or positional play are examples of where shaping from a rough version to a refined model is an effective way to learn.

Chaining

Remember how you learned to swim by initially practising the arms, then arms and legs and then arms and legs and breathing components? Or the triple-jump by developing the hop, the step and the jump before trying to piece them altogether? Chaining involves breaking a technique down into component parts so that players can work sequentially through each part. To use this method effectively, coaches need to know how the parts of the technique fit together. If a technique is too complicated to break down into parts, the shaping approach might be more beneficial to use.

For instance, it is difficult to break the basic kicking action into separate parts, so it is best learned as a whole movement. However, the development of a dribbling technique might lend itself to a chaining approach.

Chaining

When learning a dribbling technique such as the scissors, more effective learning might take place using the chaining method. The progressive learning of parts of the technique might proceed as follows:

1 **Introduce basic ball manipulation with the inside and outside of both feet.**
2 **Establish a start position and walk through the step-over-the-ball movement.**
3 **Add the touch by the other foot to take the ball away to the side.**
4 **Work on changes of pace within the sequence of movements (i.e. 'slow in – fast out'.**
5 **Add disguise with body feints and changes of direction.**

This example could include more simple and progressive steps but it shows how the movement is built up through a succession of related parts being pieced together.

These parts are learned in sequence until the chain is complete, and each part is practised as it would be performed in a refined technique.

Unlike shaping, in which initial practice promotes rough forms of the whole movement, the chaining method involves practising distinct but related parts, and then linking them together in a complete action.

Techniques do not need to be learned by using one method or the other, since chaining and shaping can be combined. For instance, once the scissors dribbling technique has been developed into a rough version through a chaining approach, shaping could be used to refine this basic action. The use of upper body feints and a double scissors leg action could be shaped into a more refined model.

Whole-part-whole

When young players are becoming interested in football they usually want to play some form of game. 'When are we having a game?' is a common question asked by most children after ten or 15 minutes of practice. In helping young players learn about the game of football, it is necessary to use simplified versions of the game (the whole) that are constructed to promote practise of new techniques or skills (the parts).

To capture players' interest and maintain their motivation, as well as providing a testing ground for new techniques and skills, a game is a useful starting point within a practice session. However, the game should be planned to provide particular challenges that require the performance of specific skills or techniques. If these skills and techniques are not performed effectively, the game can be stopped while practice of these key parts is undertaken. Once players appear to have grasped what is required they are allowed to return to the game to see how effective the practice has been.

Often called the 'isolation method', removing a part for specific practice and then putting it back into the whole, is common within teaching and coaching. But remember, the whole might not always be a full version of the game of football. With young players it is very often a small-sided game situation (e.g. three vs. three).

Too often the whole-part-whole method is used without planning by coaches who wait to see something go wrong and then decide that every player needs to practise this defective part. To work effectively, this approach needs just as much planning as shaping and chaining approaches; and games should be constructed to encourage specific skills and techniques. It will promote learning if the development of a 'part' is built around more than one practice. Providing a variety of different but related practices should encourage better understanding and maintain motivation.

Using demonstrations and providing feedback

Quote | 'A picture paints a thousand words.'

Demonstrations are a vital aid to learning for players of all abilities. When working with young players or novices, it is important that demonstrations should be:

- **Performed at the correct speed (or slowly for emphasis) and in a position where everyone can see.**

- Given in the same direction as the player will perform (not from a facing position, since this provides a mirror image and can be confusing for younger children).
- Of a higher standard than the players' current level but not necessarily an expert model.
- Accompanied by brief and clear coaching points (e.g. what to look for, how it should feel).

Children need help in knowing what to look for in a demonstration and about what they should expect to feel. For example, use of simple cues such as 'big toe' and 'little toe' when coaching dribbling and turning techniques is an effective way to help children understand what part of the foot to use. Similarly, asking children to 'scrunch your toes' when striking a ball with the laces helps them to feel the foot position and places the foot into the correct angle.

Providing feedback

Coaches are always providing some form of information to players. This is termed 'feedback' and is usually given verbally, although the use of video replays is becoming another popular feedback mechanism.

Players at all levels need time to process the results of their actions before a coach should offer additional feedback based on observation. Nevertheless, inexperienced players and young children are less able to make sense of what happened and so have a greater need for feedback from other sources. As players gain experience, they are better able to compare their own actions with previous attempts or those of other players.

Beware of the commentator's approach to giving feedback. There is a tendency for coaches to want to commentate on everything they observe – this is a commentator's job, not the coach's. Providing information after every attempt does not necessarily lead to more effective learning. Intermittent feedback is better for learning and motivation.

Providing feedback

When providing feedback to young players, coaches should:

- Give verbal feedback when working with inexperienced players.
- Keep information short and simple (KISS).
- Give the players time to process their own feedback (e.g. what the movement felt like, what was the outcome) before adding to it.
- Ask questions to check understanding and encourage problem solving (e.g. 'what happened?', What could you do next time'?).
- Encourage the players to focus on what their actions felt like rather than the outcome.
- Use feedback as praise, and reward effort as well as attainment.

Sven-Goran Eriksson with David Beckham

▩ Communication

What are the features of effective communication in coaching? What are the features of ineffective communication? List all the different methods of communicating with players including those who might have particular needs (i.e. visual or hearing impairment).

What else will improve my coaching method?

Sometimes it is the little things that make the difference, and the following list provides examples that might help your coaching method to become more successful and enjoyable for you and your players:

*   Try to know everyone's name and encourage them to learn each other's names.

*   Organize groupings of players and use of space in advance. Try to use groupings that build and progress (e.g. groups of threes can translate easily into three vs. three practices, and then six vs. six games).

*   Have a method for organizing groups that integrates players rather than segregates into friendship groups (e.g. if you want four groups, give players a number from one to four and form groups by number).

*   Identify a suitable coaching position so that you can observe effectively yet not be in the way.

*   Use a consistent stop and start command so that players respond quickly. A verbal command is more personal (e.g. 'Stop. Stand still'), but a whistle is useful when outdoors and when working with large groups.

*   Seek to have some form of contact with every player in every session.

*   Try to make practice and game situations as realistic as possible.

▩ Coaching styles

Describe the different styles of coaching you have received or observed. Which is the best style for you?

Introduction to coaching styles

How you coach is as important as what you coach. Your planning, preparation and approach to a session can be undermined if you don't adopt a style of coaching which suits the needs of the players.

Are you the bossy coach who makes all of the decisions and tells players what to do and when to do it? Perhaps you are more of a guide who shares decision making and encourages players to set their own performance targets. Most coaches lie between these two extremes, and personality, coaching philosophy and the nature of the activity influence which coaching style is most appropriate. Part of the challenge of coaching is to be able to modify coaching style to suit the needs of the learner and the situation.

With younger players and in situations where the coach needs to be aware of possible dangers (for instance, close to roads or when working with large numbers in limited space), coaches need to be more commanding because safety is a critical factor. This command style might also instil trust and confidence in players and parents, particularly if they are not familiar with practice organization and procedures. It is also useful for capturing and directing attention, for example when demonstrating a technique or set piece (e.g. 'Stop, Stand still. Watch me').

One-to-one coaching, game-related practices or working with more experienced players might favour a guided-discovery style of coaching. This style encourages more involvement from the players in their own learning by setting problems to solve and asking more questions.

For example, guided-discovery might be a more effective style to adopt when seeking to help a group of players make better use of space to retain possession of the ball. By placing restrictions on a small-sided game (for instance, where players have a maximum of two touches) or using an overload practice (for example, four players vs. two players) you will be guiding the learning situation to promote the importance of support play by players who are not in possession of the ball. In addition, players will be challenged to discover the most effective ways to retain possession by utilizing the space available.

The guided-discovery style is also a challenge to coaches because it places more importance on the learner and less on the coach to direct and control learning situations. The use of questioning is an important tool when seeking to help players take more responsibility for their own learning.

Questioning

Using questions can be a feature in both the command and guided-discovery styles of coaching. The commanding coach might check players' understanding of instructions by asking 'Does everyone know which group they are in?'. This is a closed question because it requires only a 'Yes' or 'No' response but is important for safety and organizational reasons.

The guided-discovery style invites coaches to ask more open questions to prompt problem solving ('How can you combine together to create a shooting opportunity?') or analyse their own decision making ('What made you choose to shoot rather than pass?'). When beginning to use questions in your coaching, it is helpful to prepare the questions you might ask in particular football situations. Try using questions starting with 'How?', 'What?', 'When?', 'Where?', rather than 'Why?', which tends to prompt negative responses ('Because I can't head the ball very well'), and be prepared to invite and answer questions.

If you are unsure of an appropriate question to ask, guide players' learning by using 'show me' instead of feeling the need to tell them what to do next or what should have happened. The more the players become involved in their own learning the more effectively they should progress.

Good coaches will make themselves redundant by helping players to become more self-reliant. However, the need to maintain safe practice and for coaches to feel in control of what is happening means a more commanding style is wise to adopt until experience is developed.

Positive and effective communication

Since communication is a two-way process, coaches need to be able to listen as well as talk. If instructions are unclear, problems will occur and players should be encouraged to share their ideas and thoughts with coaches, since this helps to maintain motivation and develop positive relationships.

To communicate effectively, you should try to:

- Ask questions as well as instruct, find out what motivates players, what they enjoy about football, what they need to improve, what their ambitions are, and so on.
- Listen to players, parents and other coaches (don't look away when they are speaking to you).
- Plan what you are going to say.
- Keep information and instructions short and simple.
- Avoid jargon, sarcasm and talking for the sake of it.
- Talk with players, not at them.
- Be prepared to share a joke and show you have a sense of humour.
- Be positive and build on players' strengths rather than identifying shortcomings.
- Use your voice to capture attention, emphasize a key point and show emotions (e.g. speaking quickly is often interpreted as a sign of anxiety, while talking too slowly suggestions seriousness).
- Smile and make eye contact when speaking to players and other people.

This range of communication skills takes a while to develop and might not appear naturally. Use some of your coaching sessions to practice your communication skills and ask players to provide feedback. If you don't work at your communication skills, the valuable knowledge and experiences you have might never get through to the players you coach. This can lead to motivational problems as well as lack of understanding amongst players.

Verbal communication skills

Being an effective coach does not require a megaphone or the voice of a town crier. It does require effective use of the voice so that players can hear and understand what a coach is saying. Changing the tone, pitch and speed of verbal communication will help to gain and hold players' attention regardless of the speaker's accent. Speaking quietly can bring calmness and sincerity to a situation, and planning what to say before saying it promotes a sense of authority.

When planning your coaching sessions, make a list of important instructions, key factors or questions you might seek to ask. Try to avoid too much jargon and keep information short and simple (the KISS principle). In addition, plan your positioning to ensure that everyone can see and hear you speak, and check that people understand any instructions given.

Listening and non-verbal communication skills

The majority of all communication is non-verbal and often begins with dress and appearance. Dressing scruffily and having untidy hair does not convey an attitude of caring, good preparation or personal respect. Appearing smartly and appropriately dressed in clean clothing, and being punctual, well-organized and smiling creates a picture of a more friendly, respectable and authoritative coach.

When you are coaching, you will at various times use eye contact, clapping, nodding, scowling, waving, pointing and other body movements to convey messages to people around you. Try to use them positively and to provide encouragement even though this might mean masking your inner feelings. Experienced coaches will tell you how often they have shrugged their shoulders at a player who has just shot wide, seconds after silently cursing the same player for missing the target.

Next time you say to someone 'Sorry, I didn't quite catch what you said', remember how important it is to listen. Listening and hearing are as important as talking for coaches at all levels. Try to be an active listener by paying attention to the speaker as well as the message. Make eye contact with the speaker, nod to show you understand information or questions, avoid interrupting, and be prepared to ask questions for clarification.

Motivating players

Coaches need to use a variety of strategies to motivate players of differing ages and abilities. These strategies might include:

- **Goal-setting.**
- **Providing positive feedback about performance.**
- **Using rewards.**
- **Rewarding effort, not just outcome.**
- **Focusing on success as well as winning.**
- **Making practice challenging, varied and enjoyable.**
- **Encouraging players to have some responsibility for their own development.**

Goal-setting

Goal-setting can be used to increase players' motivation and self-confidence, and reduce anxiety. By agreeing specific performance goals with each player, coaches should seek to focus attention on personal achievement, not winning.

To illustrate, the refinement of a particular technique (for example, Cruyff turn) so that it can be performed consistently well, should be more likely to enhance feelings of accomplishment than if a player contributes little to a team's win. Successfully achieving performance goals should increase the potential for a winning outcome – coaches should agree targets based on *process* rather than *product* goals.

Quote | 'If you fail to prepare, prepare to fail.'
(Chinese proverb)

Smarter goals

In using goal-setting with players, coaches should try to make goals:

- **Specific to the performance** (e.g. 'I want to stop my opponent turning with the ball in our defensive third of the pitch').
- **Measurable** (e.g. 'How often did my opponent turn with the ball?).
- **Acceptable to the player (and agreed by the coach and player).**
- **Realistic but challenging** (e.g. only in the final third of the pitch, not the whole pitch).
- **Time-phased** (e.g. during the game).
- **Exciting so that players feel a sense of achievement.**
- **Recorded to enable players and coaches to monitor progress.**

The example focuses on what a player has to do to be successful (process or performance goal) rather than the result of the game (product or outcome goal). Successful achievement of process goals should contribute positively towards overall team performance. For example, successfully stopping an opponent from turning in the defensive third of the pitch should restrict the creation of goal-scoring opportunities and allow cover to be assembled.

Based on material developed by the National Coaching Foundation (NCF) in the *Motivation and Mental Toughness Handbook* (1999)

Use of rewards

Success and enjoyment are the critical ingredients in motivating players of all ages and abilities. Planned, progressive and challenging practices are the key to this success. Rewards should be used to let players know they are doing well, not as a means of control.

A young player's involvement in junior football with clubs and schools often includes competing for trophies and the award of medals. These extrinsic rewards can provide a positive stimulus for young players and encourage them to play and practise. Nevertheless, young players should enjoy football for the fun or excitement of playing so that they will continue to participate even if they do not win trophies or receive medals.

Such extrinsic rewards have an important influence on young players' motivation and make parents very proud, but they should not become the reason for playing. They are a means to an end, not the end itself. Good coaches should encourage intrinsic motivation through challenging and exciting sessions, which incorporate winning/losing and success/failure but always leave the young player wanting to come back next session.

Very often, players respond well to praise, a smile or a pat on the back. If these gestures are accompanied by positive feedback about performance they reinforce successful practice. Positive rewards should be used to provide information, not to control players' behaviour. Threatening the slowest player with another set of shuttle runs might provoke an immediate response but it is likely to lead to a lack of trust and respect by the player.

Use of additional physical activity as a form of punishment should be discouraged. It frequently penalizes players who might benefit from extra technique practice and who might be less able than others. Young players who fail to achieve their goal should be offered remedial practice, not subjected to a form of physical punishment. In the long term this will put them off practising and playing football.

Coaches should also seek to praise effort as well as achievement, particularly with younger children. For many young players, effort is all they might be able to control so it should be rewarded, but not at the expense of skill development.

Praise followed by corrective feedback, followed by praise is a positive way of motivating players.

Quote	'Alf was very quiet and to the point. Coaches often strike up a different tone to their voice, they lecture you but Alf didn't, he'd just have a conversation and make suggestions.' (George Cohen about Sir Alf Ramsey in Barker, D. (1998) *A Biography of Sir Alf Ramsey*, Gollanz)

Resolving conflict

Conflict is unpleasant and unproductive. While we want our players and teams to have a challenging attitude and win, it should be without the negative influence that internal or external conflict brings.

Conflict may arise at any time in the highly charged arena of football. Conflict could potentially occur between any two people involved, but within your control/influence it is most likely to happen between:

- **Players in your team.**
- **Your player(s) and those in the other team.**
- **Players and match officials.**
- **You and other coaches.**
- **You and match officials.**
- **Players/you and spectators.**

As a coach you should try to calm any situation of conflict. This can be achieved in any number of ways and will require you to remain calm and not get involved.

Conflict on the field is the responsibility of the match officials/referee, but as the coach it may be your responsibility to influence a situation. This can be accomplished by speaking to players off the field, substituting a player who is in conflict with another or reading the riot act to ensure that the codes of the game are maintained. If the conflict is addressed towards you, try to take yourself out of the situation by moving away or adapting your behaviour.

Conflict between your players will not always be sorted out quickly. You may have to instigate strategies to help the team gel and either begin to like, or at least tolerate, each other. There could be times when, for the benefit of the team, you have to let perfectly good players go because of their poor interactions within the team.

Handling conflict

List a minimum of three examples of potential conflict that might arise in your coaching sessions. How, as the coach, should you handle these instances?

Summary

This chapter has provided an outline of some of the 'personal' qualities and competencies you need to develop to improve your ability as a coach, leader, communicator and conflict resolver!

The chapter will have allowed you the opportunity to develop a coaching philosophy with which you are comfortable. You will need to coach in a way that is compatable with your own personality and this chapter will have provided a guide in this respect.

Self testers

1 Which of your coaches or teachers have had the greatest effect upon you?

2 What were the qualities of the coach or teacher that had the most lasting impression upon you?

3 How would you test and prioritize your qualities as a coach?

Action plan

I want to improve my coaching style   A good start is to undertake one of The FA Coaching courses. You can also take the opportunity to watch and observe some successful coaches whose ethics and attitudes you admire. Finally, plan and practise your own coaching styles and, above all, evaluate the effectiveness of your coaching sessions.

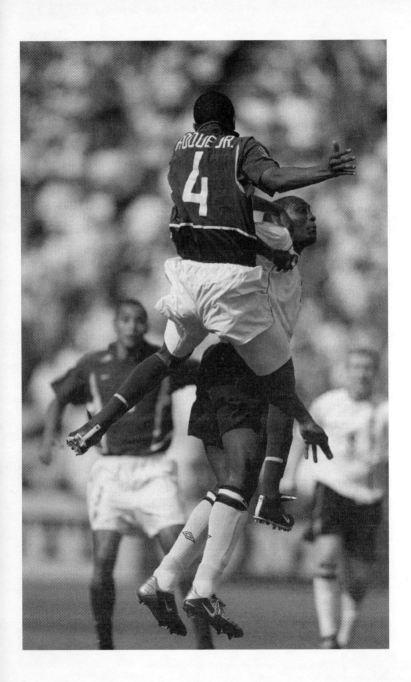

Chapter 2

Learning from successful teams

THIS CHAPTER WILL:

- Explore the 11 characteristics of successful teams.
- Outline the basics of Brazil's World Cup victories in 2002.
- Demonstrate what statistics can tell us about the successful French national teams of 1998–2000.
- Identify key aspects for you to focus upon to support your team performances.

Success in football is dependent upon a range of factors, perhaps most importantly the ability of the players available for selection, and the quality of the team's preparation and organization. The correct choice of strategy and tactics relative to the strengths and weaknesses of the team and its forthcoming opponents are also crucial. It is clear that successful teams have common characteristics.

Eleven characteristics of successful teams

In an *Insight* article in 2000, Andy Grant recorded 11 main characteristics involved in successful team performance. Successful teams are deemed to be those that have won competitions played over a number of matches and the definition does not refer to performance in single games. It is, of course, possible to win individual matches without the performance characteristics. Nevertheless, teams enjoying success over a longer period of time usually demonstrate the following qualities.

1 More possession.

Successful teams have more possession of the ball. This enables the team to:

- Control the structure of matches.
- Exploit the opposition's defensive weaknesses.
- Reduce the likelihood of conceding a goal.
- Avoid wasting energy chasing a ball to regain possession.

Analysis of successful teams shows that:

- Players in successful teams in the 1986 World Cup had more touches of the ball per possession.
- The 1994 World Cup winners, Brazil, had more time in possession of the ball and covered a greater distance with the ball in their possession.
- Successful teams in the 1998 World Cup made more passes than unsuccessful teams.

2 More attempts at goal

There is a close link between the number of attempts at goal and the number of goals scored. While there is always the possibility of a team scoring a goal from few attempts, it is unlikely that this will be successful over a number of matches. Performances by successful teams have provided evidence to support this. These teams include the 1990 World

Cup winners, West Germany; the 1994 World Cup winners, Brazil; the four 1998 World Cup semi-finalists; the 1999 Women's World Cup finalists; and the 1998–9 treble winners, Manchester United.

3 More attacking moves enter the critical attacking areas

Successful teams demonstrate a greater ability to penetrate the opposition's defence with more attacks. Entry into the goal-scoring areas is essential to score goals, with the occasional spectacular long shot. More attacking moves ending in the critical scoring area have the by-product of allowing teams to regain possession higher up the field and to win more set plays around the opponent's penalty area.

4 Attacking through the centre of the field more effectively

Penetrating the opposition's defence in central positions is considerably more likely to result in a goal than penetration on the wing. The time that defenders have to recover before a shot can be taken is reduced considerably when the attack is made centrally compared to near the touchline. The ability to penetrate through the centre of the pitch is a crucial aspect of successful team performance.

5 The ability to create scoring opportunities from possession play and direct play

Most goals are scored from attacking moves containing few passes and involving a short time in possession of the ball. However, successful teams in the 1998 World Cup also demonstrated the ability to score goals and create shooting opportunities in open play from longer periods of possession. These involved more passes than the attacking moves used by unsuccessful teams.

6 The ability to create goals and attempts at goal from regained possessions in their defensive half

The ability to create scoring opportunities in open play from attacking moves originating in the defensive half was illustrated by successful teams in recent World Cups, such as the 1998 and 2002 tournaments. This was

often the result of fast counter-attacks with players running with the ball at speed, quick inter-passing, accurate long passing and slow controlled build-ups involving defenders carrying the ball into mid-field areas.

7 Regaining possession of the ball in the attacking areas more frequently

This highlights the high work rate of players in successful teams in closing down the opposing players in possession of the ball, and the ability of the players to anticipate the ball in second-phase possession (i.e. when possession of the ball is unsecured by either team). Regaining possession in the critical scoring area is also a consequence of incisive attacking play where, after a last-ditch tackle by a defending player, the ball runs loose to another attacking player or an attacking set play is won.

8 Adopting patterns of play that involve consecutively running, dribbling and passing the ball in a forward direction

Successful teams are able to penetrate the defence by running, dribbling and/or passing the ball in a forward direction for longer consecutive sequences of play. This attacking pattern of play is characteristic of successful team performance because:

- It prevents defending players from having the time to recover.
- It shows that possession of the ball leads to penetration.
- Players receiving the ball with their back to goal have the technical ability and perceptual awareness to turn and play forward.
- The players frequently beat their opponent in one-on-one situations.

9 Using crosses to score goals and to create scoring opportunities

There are many times during a match when teams are faced with the need to penetrate a retreating, heavily numbered and balanced defence.

When there is no opportunity to attack centrally, the successful teams have demonstrated their effectiveness at exploiting the opposition out on the flanks. The use of accurate crosses with perfect timing of runs by players not in possession into the penalty box is another characteristic of successful team performance. In the 1998–9 season, Manchester United was very effective in scoring goals from crosses.

10 Making effective use of set plays

Analysis of goals scored in games over the last 40 years has revealed that set plays account for between 30–40 per cent of all goals scored. Successful teams are more effective at scoring goals and creating scoring chances from set plays. They are also better at defending set plays awarded against them.

11 Variability in performance over a number of matches

Successful teams show more variability in key aspects of performance such as the number of passes played in wide and central areas of the pitch, and in the defensive, mid-field and attacking areas. Their results suggest that such teams adapt their style of play to counteract their opponents' specific strengths.

■ Think of a successful team you admire. Objectively prioritize five characteristics of the team and justify these characteristics from data you have collected.

Case study: Brazil, 2002

Brazil has long been admired for its attractive attacking style of football. It is perhaps no coincidence that the country has won the World Cup on more occasions than any other nation. The 2002 side bore resemblance to many of Brazil's famous teams of the past in that it is packed with attack-minded, highly-skilled individuals who also play well together as a team.

Recent research by Taylor and Williams (2002) looks at the attacking play that produced the goals and attempts on goal during Brazil's games in the 2002 World Cup (see Table 1). Areas of their work include goals scored, attempts on goal, pass direction, set plays and types of assist.

Table 1 **Brazil's matches during the 2002 World Cup**

Opponent	Score	Stage	Date
Turkey	2–1	Group	3 June
China	4–0	Group	8 June
Costa Rica	5–2	Group	13 June
Belgium	2–0	2nd stage	17 June
England	2–1	Quarter-final	21 June
Turkey	1–0	Semi-final	26 June
Germany	2–0	Final	30 June

Goals scored, attempts at goal and goal-scoring efficiency

Brazil scored 18 goals and conceded only four over the course of its seven matches during the 2002 World Cup competition, outscoring its opponents by a ratio of over 4:1 (see Table 2). In contrast, in the 1998 tournament France scored 15 goals and conceded two goals.

Table 2 **Goals and attempts on goal from open and set play**

	Brazil		Opponents	
	Attempts	Goals	Attempts	Goals
Open play	65	12	45	3
Set play	37	6	36	1
Total	102	18	81	4

Brazil did not have significantly more attempts on goal (on and off target) overall than its opponents, averaging 15 attempts per game to 12 attempts by its opponents. In 1998, France averaged a similar number of attempts on goal per game (16) to Brazil whilst its opponents only averaged five attempts on goal per game. Brazil might have been less cautious defensively, offering opponents ample opportunities to score, while the team displayed excellent efficiency with regard to converting goal attempts into goals. Efficiency was fundamental to Brazil's success in the 2002 tournament.

The gulf in scoring efficiency between Brazil and its opponents is highlighted in Table 3. Brazil converted 1:6 (18 per cent) of attempts into goals, compared to only 1:20 (5 per cent) by the opposition. In the 1998 World Cup and Euro 2000 tournaments, France had a similar scoring efficiency, 1:7 (14 per cent). However, its opponents were far less efficient, producing a goal from every ten attempts (9.5 per cent).

Table 3 **Strike rate/Efficiency**

| | Brazil | | Opponents | |
Goals to attempts	%	Ratio	%	Ratio
Open play	18	1:5	7	1:15
Set play	16	1:7	3	1:36
All play	18	1:6	5	1:20

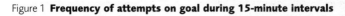

Brazil only conceded one goal during the entire tournament from a set play, despite its opponents creating 36 attempts on goal from these set plays, whereas the team scored a total of six goals from 37 set plays – a high achievement.

Figure 1 **Frequency of attempts on goal during 15-minute intervals**

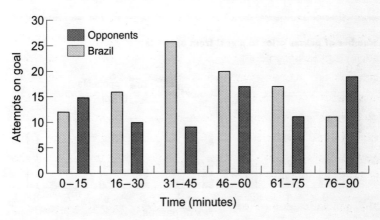

Attempts on goal at times of the game

The number of attempts on goal for Brazil and its opponents is broken down into 15-minute periods in Figure 1. Brazil had less attempts than its opponents during the opening and closing 15-minute periods, however the team appears to have dominated play, as determined by the number of attempts on goal, during the middle portion of the match.

Time in possession and the number of passes prior to a goal from open play

Time in possession prior to a goal in open play

Time (seconds)	Number of goals	%
0–5	2	17
6–10	3	25
11–15	3	25
16–20	1	8.25
21–25	1	8.25
26–30	1	8.25
31–35	0	0
35–40	1	8.25

Number of passes prior to a goal from open play

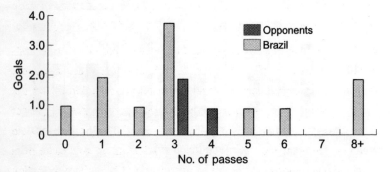

Regained possession resulting in attempts on goal and goals scored

The area of the pitch where possession leading to an attempt on goal was regained is displayed in Figure 2. Altogether, 37 of Brazil's attempts on

Figure 2 **Areas of regained possession leading to an attempt at goal during open play**

1 2	1 0	1 0	6 3	1 2	0 0
10 4	5 2	11 2	7 3	3 12	5 2
0 1	4 0	4 1	3 4	2 6	1 1

0 = Brazil
0 = Opponent

Direction of play ⟶

goal in open play came from regaining possession in the defensive half, compared to 28 attempts from regained possession in the attacking half.

Brazil were well balanced on both sides of the pitch with regard to the number of attempts at goal arising from regained possessions in wide areas. There were ten attempts on the left side and 14 on the right side.

This latter finding may highlight the unique, all-round talents of Brazil's wide players in their ability to win possession and initiate counter-attacks from any area of the field. Another interesting observation is that the highest number of regained possessions leading to attempts on goal for Brazil came from its own penalty area (ten) and the defensive mid-field area (11), whereas most of its opponents' attempts on goal came from regained possession outside Brazil's penalty area (12), perhaps indicating Brazil's tendency to be caught in possession when attempting to play the ball out from the defensive area. The area where regains resulted in goals is highlighted in Figure 3. Altogether, nine of Brazil's goals came after the team had regained possession in the defensive half of the pitch. Since the

Figure 3 **Areas of regained possession leading to a goal in open play**

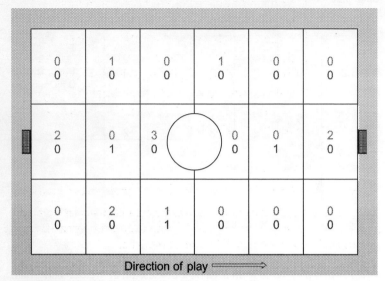

0 = Brazil
0 = Opponent

majority of these goals were scored from sequences of play involving five or less passes and lasting 6–15 seconds, this observation highlights the team's ability to play incisive attacking football, moving the ball forward quickly and decisively. Two of the remaining three goals were scored after possession was regained inside the opposition's penalty area, perhaps highlighting the quick thinking of Brazil's attacking players.

Passing

Brazil tended to pass the ball in a forward direction with occasional backward passes to change the direction of play. The ball was passed sideways infrequently. Although there were slight variations across playing positions, the emphasis on passing the ball forward rather than sideways or backwards was consistent across all players.

Quote | 'Brazil played the beautiful game emanating from an often overlooked core of mental strength and physical condition. Their much maligned defence proved stingy way beyond their reputation! Their best was far better than the rest and thankfully they did not compromise their responsibility and commitment to playing to the samba beat.' (Howard Wilkinson, FA Technical Director, 2002)

Brazil summary

- Brazil scored more than four times as many goals as its opponents.

- In open play, Brazil and its opponents created a similar number of attempts on goal but Brazil's goal to attempts on goal ratio was 1:5 compared to 1:15 for its opponents.

- Brazil conceded most attempts on goal during the first and last 15 minutes of the game, whereas it seemed to dominate the middle portion of the game.

- Brazil's goal to attempts on goal ratio at set plays was 1:7, compared to 1:36 for its opponents.

- Only one goal from set play was conceded throughout the whole tournament, while the team scored six goals from set plays.

- Brazil was most successful in creating attempts and goals from moves containing three passes. In total, nine of Brazil's goals from open play came following sequences of play containing five passes or less and lasting between 6–15 seconds. However, Brazil did score two goals from sequences of play involving eight or more passes and lasting more than 26 seconds, indicating the importance of variety in attacking play.

- The vast majority of Brazil's attempts on goal and goals scored came after the team had regained possession in the defensive half. In contrast, its opponents had more attempts at goal after regaining possession in Brazil's defensive third.

- Brazil scored seven of its 12 goals in open play from a cross.

Case study: France, 1998 and 2000

In beating Italy on 2 July 2000, France became the first nation to win the European Championship as current world champions. Horn, Williams and Grant (2000), look at factors in attacking play which led to goals scored and attempts at goal in France's games during the World Cup and Euro 2000 championships (see Table 4).

Table 4 **France's matches during the World Cup and Euro 2000 championships**

Opponent	Score	Competition	Stage	Date
South Africa	3–0	World Cup 1998	Group	12 June 1998
Saudi Arabia	4–0	World Cup 1998	Group	18 June 1998
Denmark	2–1	World Cup 1998	Group	24 June 1998
Paraguay	1–0 (aet)	World Cup 1998	Last sixteen	28 June 1998
Italy	0–0 (pens)	World Cup 1998	Quarter-final	3 July 1998
Croatia	2–1	World Cup 1998	Semi-final	8 July 1998
Brazil	3–0	World Cup 1998	Final	12 July 1998
Denmark	3–0	Euro 2000	Group	11 June 2000
Czech Republic	2–1	Euro 2000	Group	16 June 2000
Holland	2–3	Euro 2000	Group	21 June 2000
Spain	2–1	Euro 2000	Quarter-final	25 June 2000
Portugal	2–1 (aet)	Euro 2000	Semi-final	28 June 2000
Italy	2–1 (aet)	Euro 2000	Final	2 July 2000

aet = after extra time
pens = penalties

France scored a goal for every seven attempts at goal in open play (13.7 per cent), while the opponents scored a goal for every 28 attempts at goal (3.6 per cent). Of all attempts at goal on target in open play, France scored in more than one in four attempts (27.4 per cent of the time), against just one in 13 attempts (7.7 per cent) for its opponents. France only conceded two goals from open play in both tournaments combined.

Analysis of goals scored, attempts at goal and goal-scoring efficiency

France outscored its opponents in the two tournaments at a rate of over three to one, netting 28 to the opposition's nine goals. This difference was especially notable in World Cup 1998 where France scored 15 goals and conceded only two (see Table 5). In Euro 2000, where it could be argued that the opposition was consistently stronger in every game, France still outscored its opponents by 13 goals to seven.

Table 5 **Goals scored from open and set play (goals from penalty shoot-outs not included)**

	France		Opponents	
	World Cup 1998 (n = 7)	Euro 2000 (n = 6)	World Cup 1998 (n = 7)	Euro 2000 (n = 6)
Open play	8	9	1	1
Free kick	0	2	0	1
Corner	5	1	0	1
Throw-in	1	0	0	2
Penalty	1	1	1	2
Sub-total	15	13	2	7
Total	**28**		**9**	

n = number of games

The ability of France to dominate its opponents so clearly in terms of goals scored raises the question of whether the team scored more goals by simply creating more attempts at goal, or through a greater rate of efficiency or strike rate. Table 7 shows that France created a total of 200 strikes on goal, while allowing its opponents only 95 attempts. Of these, Table 6 shows that France had 94 attempts on target, versus only 44 by the opponents. In terms of efficiency, when all types of play are

Table 6 **Attempts at goal on target (including goals) from open and set plays**

	France		Opponents	
	World Cup 1998 (n = 7)	Euro 2000 (n = 6)	World Cup 1998 (n = 7)	Euro 2000 (n = 6)
Open play	35	27	8	18
Free kick	7	7	3	5
Corner	8	2	1	1
Throw-in	3	3	2	3
Penalty	1	1	1	2
Sub-total	54	40	15	29
Total	94		44	

n = number of games

Table 7 **Total attempts at goal (on and off target, including goals)**

	France		Opponents	
	World Cup 1998 (n = 7)	Euro 2000 (n = 6)	World Cup 1998 (n = 7)	Euro 2000 (n = 6)
Open play	76	48	21	35
Free kick	16	22	7	11
Corner	15	10	2	4
Throw-in	7	4	5	6
Penalty	1	1	1	3
Sub-total	115	85	36	59
Total	200		95	

n = number of games

Table 8 **Strike rate/Efficiency for France and its opponents**

	All play			Open play	
Team	% of all attempts on goal which were on target	% of all attempts on goal which resulted in a goal	% of attempts on target which resulted in a goal	% of all attempts at goal from open play which resulted in a goal	% of attempts at goal on target from open play which resulted in a goal
France	47.0	14.0 (1:7)	29.8 (1:3)	13.7 (1:7)	27.4 (1:4)
Opponents	46.3	9.5 (1:10)	20.5 (1:5)	3.6 (1:28)	7.7 (1:13)

considered, Table 8 shows that France was not significantly more prolific than its opponents. When open play is considered, a key ingredient to France's success becomes apparent. Although analysis of open play provides the greatest contrast between France and its opponents, the European and World Champions also employed set plays more effectively (Tables 5, 6 and 7). France's consistent attacking play generated an abundance of set plays in dangerous areas. This resulted in three times as many attempts on goal from set plays in comparison to the opponents. From these, France scored 11 set-play goals, while conceding only seven. Corners were particularly effective as they resulted in six goals, two of which came in the World Cup Final. Defensively, however, France showed great organization at set plays, conceding only two attempts on target from corners in both tournaments combined.

Time in possession and number of passes prior to a goal from open play

Time in possession prior to goal scored in open play

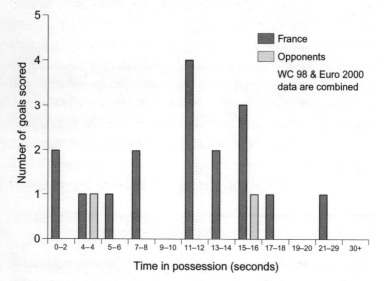

Number of passes prior to a goal being scored from open play

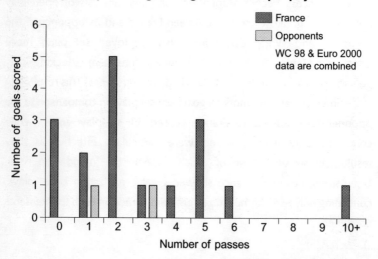

Regained possession resulting in attempts on target and goals scored in open play

Figure 4 shows the area of the field in which possession was regained prior to an attempt at goal on target in open play. France shows an exact balance of 31 in each half. This reveals many facts. First, the players show the ability to not only win the ball all over the field, but also to initiate successful moves from any position. The technical ability of the French squad in all positions is highlighted. Second, since most attempts on goal came from five or less passes, and in possessions of fairly short duration, it shows the ability of all players to make incisive passes, and carry the ball forward at speed. In creating attempts on goal, the French team also shows balance from left to right, with 11 regained possessions on each side resulting in attempts at goal on target. The clear majority of regained

Figure 4 **Regained possessions resulting in an attempt at goal on target from open play in all French matches in the tournaments**

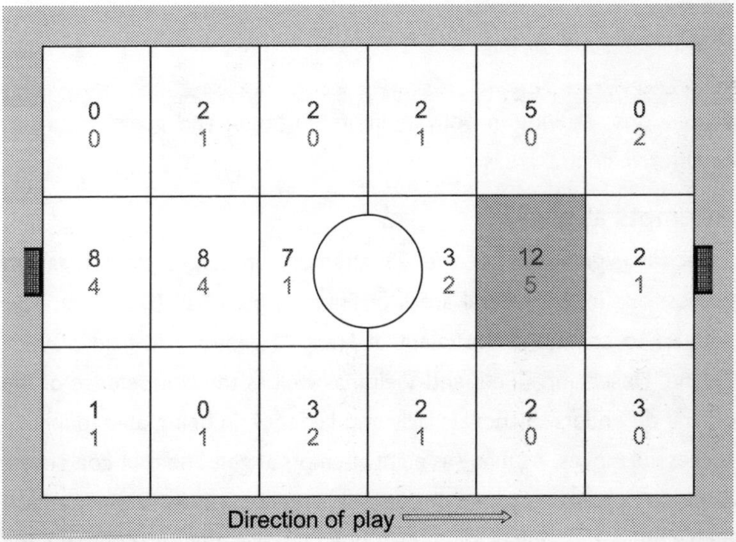

Direction of play ⟹

0 = France
0 = Opponent

Figure 5 **Regained possessions resulting in a goal from open play in all French matches in the tournaments**

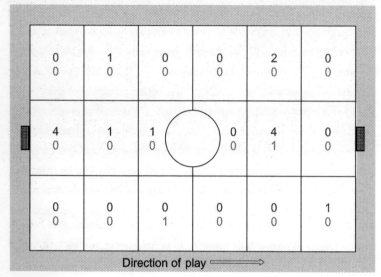

Direction of play ⟹

0 = France
0 = Opponent

possessions resulting in both attempts on target and goals (Figure 5) occurred in central areas.

Attempts at goal

Especially significant are the 23 attempts on target from regained possessions in the central areas of France's own half (Figure 4). This appears to commend the talent of France's central mid-field players, Zidane, Deschamps, Petit and Vieira, as well as the competence of the central defenders, Blanc, Desailly and Lebeouf, in being able to initiate successful moves. As many as eight attempts at goal and four goals came from possession regained inside the French penalty area, perhaps highlighting the outstanding distribution skills demonstrated by the French goalkeeper, Barthez. This is a feature regarded by many as a

necessity in successful international teams. In addition, the French defence allowed the opposition to score only one goal from regained possession in the final third in both competitions combined.

Figure 6 shows the origin of assists to goals scored in open play. France's relatively narrow attacking play is highlighted by 13 of its 16 goals coming from assists in central areas. The shaded zone is shown to be a key area, providing the most assists, one more than the penalty area.

France Summary

- In open play, France scored more than eight times as many goals as its opponents.
- France created twice as many total attempts on goal as did the opponents.
- France was more efficient than opponents in open play, scoring at a rate of one goal for every four attempts on target, against its opponents' one for every 13 attempts.
- In set plays, France outperformed the opposition, and was particularly successful at corners.

- France showed the ability to regain possession and create an attempt on target equally well from the attacking and defending half of the field.

- France conceded only one goal from the loss of possession in its own half in both tournaments combined.

- The majority of France's attempts at goal came from assists in central attacking areas just outside the penalty area.

Figure 6 **The origin of assists to goals scored (includes pass, start of dribble, and area of regained possession if unassisted) in all French matches in the tournaments**

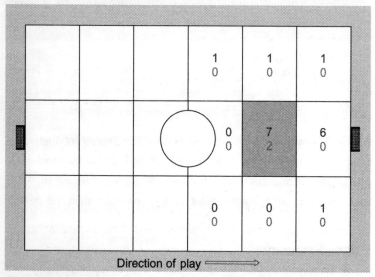

Direction of play ⟹

0 = France
0 = Opponent

Summary

- Teams are successful most notably because they have more quality players than their opposition.

- When the quality of players is evenly spread, certain characteristics of successful teams will emerge.

- Players in successful teams will be able to dominate offensively and defensively against their opposite numbers on the opposing team.

Self testers

1 List five characteristics of successful teams.

2 Prioritize the three aspects of the success of France or Brazil in the World Cups of 1998 or 2002.

3 What would be the three major aspects of your defensive strategy if your team was playing against Brazil?

Action plan

Choose three of the defining characteristics of successful teams and apply these measurements to the team you coach. For the three chosen characteristics, can you or a colleague analyse whether you outscore your opposition over a period of three games? Share your findings with your players.

References

Grant, A. (2000) *Eleven Key Characteristics of Successful Team Performance*, Insight 4 (3) pp. 26–7

Taylor, S., Williams, M. (2002) *A Quantitative Analysis of Brazil's Performances*, Insight (5) 4 p. 35

Grant, A., Horn, R., Williams, M. (2000) *Analysis of France in World Cup 1998 and Euro 2000*, Insight (4) 1 pp. 40–3

Chapter 3

Team strategies

> THIS CHAPTER WILL:
> - Outline the three key 'moments' in a game.
> - Explain the principles of play as they relate to each 'moment'.
> - Demonstrate simple practices for each 'moment'.
> - Provide challenges for your players to practise and enjoy!

Within the area of team strategies, the importance of systems of play is exaggerated. No system will overcome inaccurate passing or inaccurate shooting. No system caters for players who will not support each other or for players who will not or cannot run. Systems of play are concerned with the arrangement of the players on the field of play. The number of permutations of these players, however, is quite small. Most managers and coaches would agree that there are three groups:

1   Back players.
2   Mid-field players.
3   Forward players.

The fact of the matter is that two teams can play with the same system, for example, four back players, three mid-field players and three forward players, and yet play in a completely different way. Why? Because the players will be different and will be given different instructions. It is possible for one manager to instruct their full-backs to look constantly for opportunities to move forward in advance of the ball. It is possible for the opposing manager to instruct their full-backs never to move forward in advance of the ball. It is possible for one manager to arrange their forward players to play with wingers and for the opposing manager to arrange to play without wingers. The eventual pattern and arrangement will be very different. When teams lose it is usually not because they played 4-3-3 instead of some other system, it is most frequently because the team failed to perform well during one or more of the three key moments of the game. For the player, these are:

1 **When my team has possession of the ball.**
2 **When my team does not have possession of the ball.**
3 **When possession changes from team to team.**

Note that the number of times possession changes from one team to another is quite frequent.

It is unfair to the spectator if we infer that the whole business of tactics is really systems of play. If the great mass of spectators is to enjoy football more, we must help them to understand more and, therefore, appreciate more about the game.

As far as teams are concerned, managers and coaches should understand that lack of clarity leads to lack of understanding, and lack of understanding leads to lack of agreement, and lack of agreement spells disunity and disaster. Football is an exciting and player-focused game,

with the ball frequently changing hands. The amount of time a player is actually in possession is only a small fraction of the overall 90 minutes of playing time. A team needs a strategy for the three key moments relating to possession of the ball.

How could this affect me?
The player's responsibility in each key moment

The relevance of each key moment for the player will largely depend on the number of attackers and defenders in any game situation, related to the distance from goal and the pressure on the player with the ball. However, there are a few simple possible responsibilities for the player. These are listed in the box overleaf together with the principle of play that is most appropriate for that moment for that situation. Each principle will be most applicable to a particular moment.

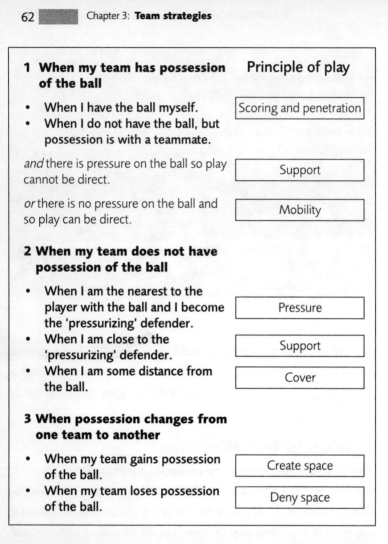

1 When my team has possession of the ball

Principle of play

- When I have the ball myself.
- When I do not have the ball, but possession is with a teammate.

Scoring and penetration

and there is pressure on the ball so play cannot be direct.

Support

or there is no pressure on the ball and so play can be direct.

Mobility

2 When my team does not have possession of the ball

- When I am the nearest to the player with the ball and I become the 'pressurizing' defender.

Pressure

- When I am close to the 'pressurizing' defender.

Support

- When I am some distance from the ball.

Cover

3 When possession changes from one team to another

- When my team gains possession of the ball.

Create space

- When my team loses possession of the ball.

Deny space

Statistic

At the very highest levels of the game, studies of the World Cup Finals have shown that possession changes on average **four** times a minute.

For example:

- 'Creating space' makes attacking easier if it is sought the moment possession is gained.

- Defending is easier if a team 'denies space' the moment immediately following loss of possession.

- 'Applying pressure' refers to the defender 'nearest' the ball and 'support' to the next nearest; 'cover' refers to those defenders farthest away from the ball.

Quote	'We believe in striking quickly from defence. A team is most vulnerable when it has just failed in attack. It is difficult to generalize but generally the second pass out of defence I would regard as the most vital.' (Sir Alf Ramsey)

Your players will need to practise decision making. Having considered the range of principles they should:

- **Test the options.**
- **Remember the consequences of their action for the future.**
- **Know what to do when a similar problem arises.**

The use of open-ended questions will be of benefit to your players. In addition, the use of questions designed to put the attacker in the defender's shoes (i.e. If you were defending what would you do?) and vice versa is also useful. Overall, the use of key moments and principles of play will help your players to develop a good team understanding. Figure 7 illustrates the relationship between principles of play and their appropriate key moment within the game.

The principles prevail under whichever tactics the coach decides to adopt. If the players understand their strategic objectives for each of the

Figure 7 **Principles of play and their key moments in the game**

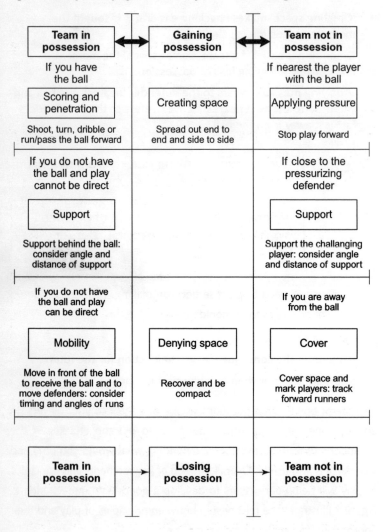

three key moments, they will be able to adapt to the most tactical formations.

Here are some practices to help your team to develop an understanding of the strategies to employ. Please ensure that the area to be used is safe, and that the players wear appropriate footwear and shin guards.

Team in possession

For the players to maintain and increase the momentum of an attack to increase the success of the attack.

Exercise A

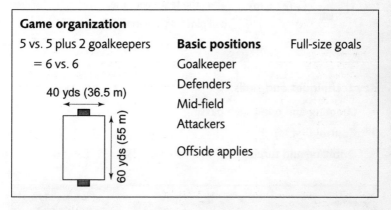

Game organization

5 vs. 5 plus 2 goalkeepers
= 6 vs. 6

40 yds (36.5 m)

60 yds (55 m)

Basic positions

Goalkeeper

Defenders

Mid-field

Attackers

Offside applies

Full-size goals

Questions to ask your players (answers in *italics*):

- Why, how and when to create space? *Why? Space =Time = Better skilled decisions; How? Move away from the ball; When? As soon as possession changes.*

- Why is it important to increase the momentum of attacks? *To avoid defenders recovering.*

- How to maintain and increase the momentum? *Shoot, dribble and one-touch passing (not passing across the field).*

- When to shoot? *Whenever possible.*

- When to dribble and shoot? *When there is space: dribble to create shooting opportunities.*

- When to use one-touch passing? *When there is insufficient space to dribble and shoot.*

Development

6 vs. 6 plus 2 goalkeepers   3 vs. 3 in each half.   Full-size goals
= 7 vs. 7

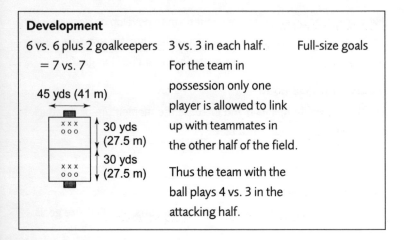

45 yds (41 m)

30 yds (27.5 m)

30 yds (27.5 m)

For the team in possession only one player is allowed to link up with teammates in the other half of the field.

Thus the team with the ball plays 4 vs. 3 in the attacking half.

Key techniques and skills:

- Shooting and one-touch passing.
- Control first touch.
- Dribbling and turning.

Exercise B

For the players to understand how to combine to create space as a team.

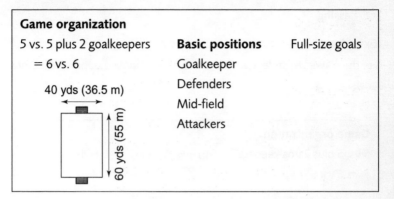

Game organization

5 vs. 5 plus 2 goalkeepers = 6 vs. 6

40 yds (36.5 m)

60 yds (55 m)

Basic positions

Goalkeeper

Defenders

Mid-field

Attackers

Full-size goals

Questions to ask your players (answers in *italics*):

* Why do we need to create space? See Task A.

* In what other ways, other than spreading out, can we create space? *Change direction of play – one-touch play.*

* Why change the direction of play? *From an area of less space and high pressure to an area of more space and less pressure.*

* How can you change the direction of play? *Cross-over runs. Cross-field passes. Reverse passes.*

* When should you play one touch? *When there is no space to dribble or shoot.*

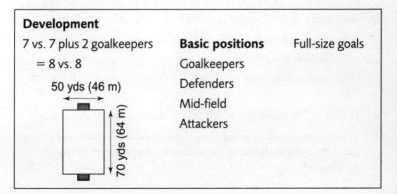

Development

7 vs. 7 plus 2 goalkeepers = 8 vs. 8

50 yds (46 m)

70 yds (64 m)

Basic positions

Goalkeepers

Defenders

Mid-field

Attackers

Full-size goals

Key techniques and skills:

- Control.
- Passing.

Exercise C

For the players to understand how to convert shooting opportunities into goals.

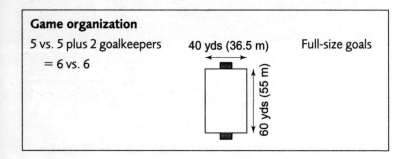

Game organization

5 vs. 5 plus 2 goalkeepers = 6 vs. 6

40 yds (36.5 m)

Full-size goals

60 yds (55 m)

Questions to ask your players (answers in *italics*):

- What percentage of opportunities were missed?
- Which shots are likely to be more effective? Low or high? *Low.*
- Why? *More difficult for the goalkeeper.*
- What will shots off target at the far post be more likely to produce than shots off target at the near post? *Rebounds and secondary scoring opportunities.*
- Which type of shots are most likely to produce rebounds? *Low shots across the goal.*
- How do you keep the ball low? *Hit through the middle of the ball.*
- Which is the more important, accuracy or power? *Accuracy.*
- Whenever possible, what should be observed before selecting the appropriate shooting technique? *The position of the goalkeeper.*

Key techniques and skills:

- Shooting.

Team not in possession

Exercise A

For the players to understand their defensive responsibilities when defending the goal.

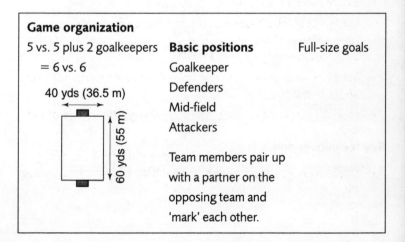

Game organization

5 vs. 5 plus 2 goalkeepers **Basic positions** Full-size goals
= 6 vs. 6 Goalkeeper

40 yds (36.5 m) Defenders

Mid-field

60 yds (55 m) Attackers

Team members pair up
with a partner on the
opposing team and
'mark' each other.

Questions to ask your players (answers in *italics*):

- Where do the opposition wish to play the ball? *Forward and behind our defence.*

- Should you, therefore, mark the player from in front or behind? *Cover space behind him/her in order to be first to the ball if played into space and to make the ground up if the ball is played to their feet.*

- What do you need to watch? *The ball and your immediate opponent – avoid watching only the ball.*

- How will you cover space, mark your opponent if he/she gets the ball, and stay between the ball and the goal you are defending? *Inside the triangle between the ball, the goal and your nearest opponent.*

- Why is it important to track runners? *So that they do not move into space and can easily dribble, shoot or pass forward.*

- When will you not track runners? *When you are drawn out of a good defending position, away from goal to an inferior defending position.*

Development

7 vs. 7 plus 2 goalkeepers   **Basic positions**   Full-size goals

= 8 vs. 8   Goalkeeper

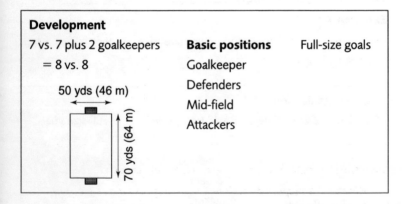

50 yds (46 m)   Defenders

Mid-field

Attackers

70 yds (64 m)

Key techniques and skills:

- Challenging for the ball, supporting, cover and balance.

Exercise B

For the players to understand the importance of pressurizing.

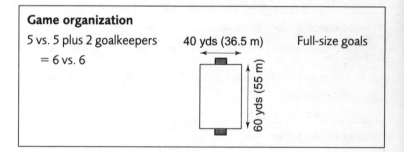

Game organization

5 vs. 5 plus 2 goalkeepers = 6 vs. 6   40 yds (36.5 m)   Full-size goals

60 yds (55 m)

Questions to ask your players (answers in *italics*):

- What must players do before they can pressurize? *Recover behind the ball.*

- Why exert pressure on the ball? *To stop shots and forward play.*

- Who should exert pressure? *The nearest defender along the line to goal.*

- Along which line should players pressurize? *Ball and goal.*

- At what speed should defenders approach? *Fast then slow.*
- How do defenders gain the initiative? *By feinting to tackle.*
- Why is it important to:
  - Watch the ball?
  - Stay on one's feet?
- When to challenge? *When the ball is outside the playing distance of the attacker.*

Development

7 vs. 7 plus 2 goalkeepers   50 yds (46 m)   Full-size goals

= 8 vs. 8

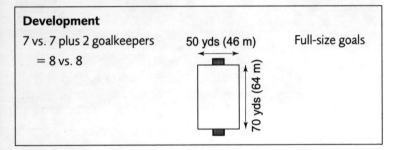

Key techniques and skills:

- Challenging for the ball, tackling, supporting and cover.
- Goalkeeping/Communication.

Exercise C

For the team as a whole to understand the need to keep the opponents' play in front of them.

Game organization

6 vs. 6   No players in the   Full-size goals

No goalkeepers   10 × 10 grid.

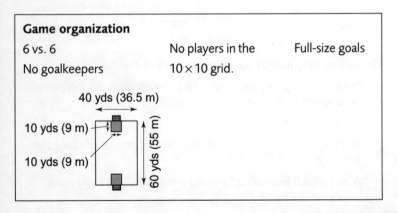

Questions to ask your players. As a coach, could you answer these?

- How, when and why to recover?
- How, when, why and where to pressurize?
- How, when and why to support the challenging player?
- How do you prevent opponents turning with the ball?
- Why is it important to watch the player with the ball and your immediate opponent?
- Can you mark too closely?
- What would be a comfortable distance?
- When do you challenge for the ball?

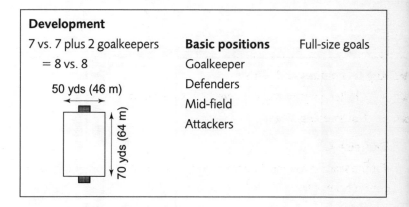

Development

7 vs. 7 plus 2 goalkeepers = 8 vs. 8

50 yds (46 m)

70 yds (64 m)

Basic positions   Full-size goals
Goalkeeper
Defenders
Mid-field
Attackers

Key techniques and skills:

- Recovery 'goalside' of the ball.
- Pressurizing the player in possession.
- Challenging for the ball.

The moment that possession changes – the 'turnover'

How to create space or deny space

Playing at the 'turnover' – the steal and strike.

Organization:

- Three zones coned off as indicated in Figure 8.
- Three Os and three Xs in each zone and two goalkeepers.
- The ball must be played through the mid-field zone.
- Touches should not be restricted.
- One mid-field player can break into the attacking zone.

Figure 8

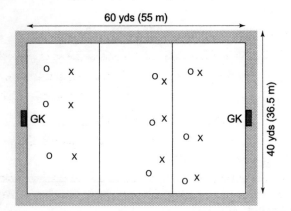

Objectives:

- To force a turnover in the tighter mid-field zone.
- To create a goal-scoring opportunity as quickly as possible.
- To utilize the imbalance of the opposition if possession is regained in the defensive zone. Play forward quickly and mid-field players create depth and angles to allow the momentum of the attack to continue forward. Then support front players and create a switch strike on opposing goal.

Opportunities:

- To coach and develop the attitude to striking out from a defensive mode.

- To emphasize the importance of finishing each attack with a strike on goal, thereby minimizing the risk of being hit while unbalanced.

- Develop movement around the box to allow for penetration and striking at goal.

Secondary coaching possibilities:

- To coach mid-field players angles of meeting up and creating depth in the mid-field. Possibly running away opponents.

- Strikes at goal can be timed from turnover but this takes away the possibility of a secondary counter-strike.

Challenges

The purpose of the following eight tasks is to set your players simple challenges for which they, amongst themselves, must work out the strategy they will deploy. The recommended procedure is as follows:

1 Give one team (e.g. Team A) the challenge.

2 The other team (e.g. Team B) is also made aware of the challenge given to Team A.

3 Allow two to three minutes for the teams to discuss which strategy they will use, together with the positional deployment of players.

4 A simple format to assist in development of strategy would be:

- What are our team's strengths and weaknesses?

- What are the opposition's strengths and weaknesses?

5 Each team should tell the coach their proposed strategy and tactics.

6 Play should commence – all challenges should indicate how many minutes remain in the game until full-time (e.g. 10/15 minutes to go).

7 **Play ceases and the teams review:**
- **What they had decided to attempt.**
- **Their assessment of its success.**
- **Reasons for success/failure.**
- **Amendments, if any, if they were given the same challenge again.**

The challenges can be combined together and may be added to by suggestions from coach and players. Please use as much imagination as possible.

▓ Choose one or two of the following challenges for your players and ask **them** to work out and action their responses.

Challenge 1

The score is 1–1 and the rules of your cup competition stipulate that the next goal is the winning goal for whichever team score it. How does your team attack and defend?

Challenge 2

Your team has one player more than the opposition. How will you take advantage of this situation? What will be your team's attacking and defensive tactics? The score is 3–0 in your favour.

Challenge 3

Your team has one player less than the opposition. What will be your team's attacking and defensive tactics? The score is 1–1.

Challenge 4

The score is 1–1 in a league competition where a win or draw allows your team to win the championship. Outline how you intend to attack and defend to win the championship. The opponents need to win the game to avoid relegation.

Challenge 5

Your team is 3–0 ahead in a knock-out cup competition match with 20 minutes to go, but with one player less than the opposition. Outline how your team will play out the last 20 minutes.

Challenge 6

The competition involves home and away legs. In the event of an aggregate draw over both legs, 'away' goals will count double. You are losing 1–2 in the first leg with 20 minutes to go. How will you attack and defend the last 20 minutes?

Challenge 7

In the same competition as Challenge 6, the score in the second leg on your home pitch is 3–2 on the night, 4–3 to your team on aggregate. Another goal for the opposition, however, to make the score 4–4 will put the opponents through on the 'away' goals rule. How does your team attack and defend for the last 20 minutes?

Challenge 8

Going into the last Saturday of the football season, your team is top of the league on goal difference above the team below by one goal. With 20 minutes to go, your team is losing 0–1. News comes through on the radio that the team below you is also losing 0–1. If the scores remain the same at the end of play, your team will win the league, but the radio commentator at the other game feels sure your rivals will equalize. How does your team attack and defend for the last 20 minutes?

Football strategy is concerned with three critical moments. What do we do as individuals and as a team: When our team has the ball? When the opposition has the ball? The moment the ball changes possession?

Movement of players when possession changes

Successful teams are noted for their effectiveness at the critical moment the ball changes possession. Quick-thinking players in possession of the ball can change the course of a game, just as quick-thinking defenders near the ball can quickly eliminate danger. As a team, let all the players in the team know they are being watched and check that:

- When the team gains possession, they generally move away from the ball to create space and open angles through which to play the ball.

- When the team loses possession of the ball they generally move towards the ball to reduce space and restrict angles through which the opposition can play the ball.

- Test your players with simple questions to ensure they understand their role for each of the three key moments.

Summary

- This chapter has outlined the three key 'moments' in a game.

- This chapter has shown how simple practices can develop your players' understanding of the requirements of these 'moments'.

Self testers

1 At the highest level of the game, how often on average does possession change each minute?

2 What do you believe are the most critical moments for a team?

3 Will your players increase their understanding more effectively by you telling them what to do or by involving them in more decision making?

Action plan

During practice sessions:

- observe your players furthest away from the ball and let them know that you are going to watch to see how the players react.

- observe the players nearest the ball to see how they react.

- observe the player who gains possession to see how he/she reacts.

Chapter 4

Squad attacking practices

THIS CHAPTER WILL:

- Offer advice on how to organize squad practices to help your team to attack.
- Provide key points for you to observe.
- Give suggestions for progression which allow development of these practices with simple adjustments.

Organization of your coaching sessions

Ask yourself the following questions:

1 How many players are involved?

2 How are they arranged?

3 What are the dimensions of the area being used?

4 How many footballs do I need? Do I need bibs? Who needs bibs?

5 What other equipment is necessary?

6 Where is my best coaching position?

7   How do I tend to start the practice?

8   What are the rules of the practice?

9   Is it safe?

10 What is the session about? Attacking, defending, shooting, crossing?

11 What are the 'key factors' of the session?

12 What is the logical order of those 'key factors'?

13 What do I want to see happening as a result of my session?

When the session is underway, ask yourself if you could:

1   Make sure the game is in an appropriate area once practice starts.

2   Keep the game flowing as much as possible.

3   Structure the game if needed.

4   Use and coach on both sides of the field.

5   Praise and encourage.

6   Look away from the ball.

7   Check coach-related elements once you have worked successfully on your main theme.

8   Involve the players by asking them to solve a problem that may have arisen.

9   Show demonstrations whenever possible.

How could these sessions progress? Could you adjust the following?

N Number of players.

E Equipment, e.g. number of goals.

A Area size.

T Task.

| **Quote** | 'I like my players to be under coached but over practised!' (Dario Gradi, Manager of Crewe Alexander, FC-FA Managers and Coaches Course, May 2003) |

A variety of conditions can be placed on any practice or game depending on the aims. These include:

- **Limited touches.**
- **Player-to-player marking.**
- **Use of zones to encourage movement.**
- **Extra goals.**
- **Extra balls.**
- **Minimum number of passes before moving to a different zone (or scoring).**
- **Time limits.**
- **Modified playing area.**

Each condition is used to encourage players to practise certain skills in a game-like situation. The skill of the coach is in selecting which conditions to apply and adapting them if they are not working. If successful, the coach will create many perfect opportunities to coach the theme of the day.

This chapter provides 16 practices for you to use with your team. Please ensure that players wear the appropriate footwear and also wear shin guards for all parts in the practices. Make sure that the environment is safe for the players to practise. Avoid loose footballs distracting the players.

As well as being game related, these activities are fun! The players should be active, easily engaged and enthusiastic, which means they are better able to learn and progress.

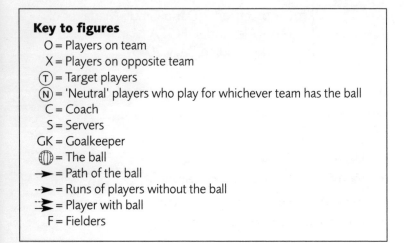

Key to figures

O = Players on team

X = Players on opposite team

(T) = Target players

(N) = 'Neutral' players who play for whichever team has the ball

C = Coach

S = Servers

GK = Goalkeeper

= The ball

—➤ = Path of the ball

··➤ = Runs of players without the ball

⫶➤ = Player with ball

F = Fielders

Development of passing and movement organization

Practice 1: Quick passing (Figure 9)

Organization

1   5 vs. 3 (25 yards × 18 yards (23 m × 16.5 m), approximately).

2   Five Xs in possession vs. three Os.

3   Other two Os remain on end line until three Os regain possession, then two Os join three Os to make five Os vs. three Xs as two Xs step back to end line until three Xs regain possession.

Figure 9

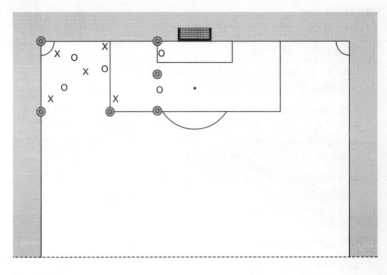

Key factors

1 Play with head up.
2 Control away from the opponent.
3 One-touch passing.
4 Spread out.

Practice 2: Passing and movement (Figure 10)

Organization

1 3 vs. 3 plus one neutral player in each zone of 25 yards (23 m) × 30 yards (27.4 m).

2 Two target players – one behind each line at a distance of 6 yards (5.5 m) from the end line.

3 The team in possession to play in one zone to pass the ball across the free zone to teammates who attempt to pass to the mobile target player: they receive possession from him/her in order to play back across the zone.

4 Neutral players play with the team in possession and do not defend.

Key factors

1 Spreading out as a team when in possession.

2 Support for the player in possession of the ball.

3 Pass forward and control the ball forward wherever possible.

4 Pass and receive, using the least number of touches possible.

Figure 10

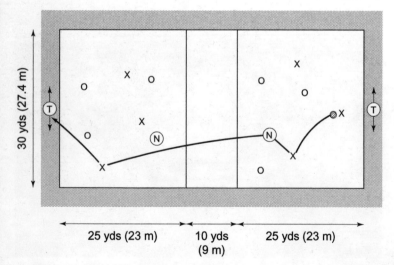

Coaches are key to the establishment of ethics in football.

When training, try and have some contact with every player in every session.

Share your coaching principles with players, parents, club members and fellow coaches so that they clearly understand your beliefs and motives.

Dribbling is an important part of the game in the attacking third and most teams could boost their goals tally simply by dribbling more in advanced positions.

In the 2002 World Cup almost half of all goals came directly or indirectly from a set play.

The more attempts on goal your team manages, the more chances they have to score!

Practice 3: Pass and move (Figure 11)

Organization

1 8 vs. 8 plus two neutral players in an area of 70 yards (64 m) × 60 yards (55 m) creates 10 vs. 8 in possession.

2 Player to score by running with the ball over the end lines.

3 The team in possession, if under pressure, may drop a player behind the end line in order to retain possession – no defending player may follow. If one player drops behind the line, a second must do so to assist player one.

Key factors

1 Width and depth for the attacking team.

2 Composure in possession.

3 Movement ahead of, and around the player in possession.

4 Pass quality to marked and unmarked players.

5 Run to, and pass-through spaces.

Figure 11

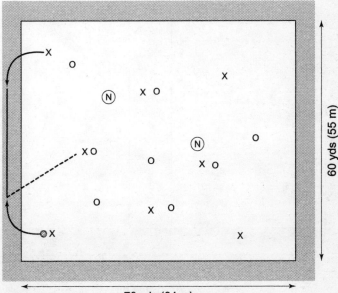

Practice 4: Play through mid-field (Figure 12)

Organization

1 As shown.

2 10 vs. 10 including goalkeepers.

Aim

To encourage passing through mid-field, X1s must play to X2s when in possession and not play long direct to X3 when the ball is with X2s. One X1 can overload the middle zone to create 4 vs. 3. X2s then look to attack the goals linking with X3s. Two X2s can overload the attacking zone to create 4 vs. 4. No Os can play outside their designated zone.

Key factors

1 Create space.

2 Support the player in possession.

3 Look to play through defenders.

Figure 12

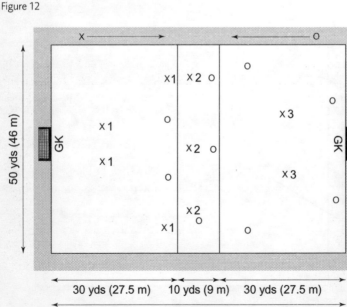

Best Practice The organization in Practice 4, relates better to the 4–3–3 and gives better positional interchange!

Practice 5: 'Three goals' (Figure 13)

Organization

1 One player behind three small goals using markers 3 yards apart.

2 A goal cannot be scored when player X is standing behind any one goal (player X tries to run behind all three goals to stop team O from scoring).

3 Size of a playing area to suit number of players but 40 × 60 yards suitable for 6 vs. 6.

Key factors

1 To encourage quick change of direction and penetration.

2 Try to eliminate the sweeper.

3 Movement from opposite side of the field.

Figure 13

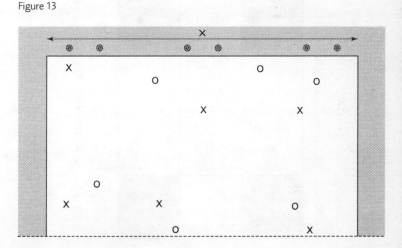

Practice 6: Target players (Figure 14)

Organization

1   The practice takes place on a grid measuring 40 yards (36.5 m)
    by 30 yards (27.5 m).

2   Three X players are opposing three O players, and at each
    corner of the grid there is a target player.

3   On each side of the grid, but outside the playing area, there are
    extra players, Ys, who can combine with whichever team is in
    possession of the ball by receiving the ball and playing it to
    their advantage.

4   The Y players can move along the touchline but they cannot
    move into the grid.

In practice, the X players are in possession of the ball and their objective
is to reach either T1 or T2 (see Figure 14). In order to prevent two of the
defending players from retreating and marking the two target players, it

Figure 14

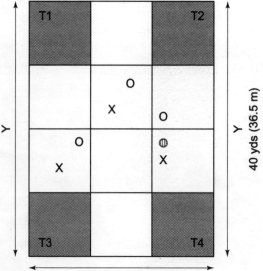

30 yds (27.5 m)

is sensible to debar both defenders and attackers from entering the shaded areas.

Once the ball has reached, for example, T1, the player passes the ball across the pitch to T2. The players position themselves in order to continue the practice in the opposite direction. If the X players have succeeded in playing to the T players, then the T player will play the ball to an X player.

The practice is physically demanding and short, but intensive periods of practice are recommended. It will be noted, however, that there are six players on the pitch and six players off the pitch. Periods of rest are achieved, therefore, by the groups changing over. The value of the practice is that it can be conditioned to achieve any type of pass or movement, for example:

- **Play is conditioned to two touches.**
- **Play is conditioned to one touch.**
- **All passes must be on the ground.**

- The target must be hit from passes made inside the attackers' defending half of the pitch. If the passes are high, they must pitch in the target player's square.

- Passes must be followed by a diagonal run.

- Passes must be followed by an overlap run.

- Attackers must respond to player-to-player marking by cross-over plays.

Any one condition should only be enforced for a short period of time and the practice should end with a period of unrestricted play.

Key factors

1 Find or create space.

2 Look forward.

3 Run forward to help the player on the ball.

4 Pass forward to the target players as quickly as possible.

Practice 7: Passing and pressurizing (Figure 15)

Organization

1 Three teams – blues, whites, reds – can be any equal numbers.

2 Balls around the side of the pitch, allowing continuity.

3 White team starts as defenders, red and blue teams are up in possession – whichever team loses possession becomes defenders and the defenders join in with the attacking side.

4 There are always 12 attackers and six defenders (or could be 5 vs. 10, 7 vs. 14 etc.).

5 Practice needs to be continuous for 15–20 minutes maximum.

Key factors

1 Keep possession.

2 Work hard to win the ball back out of possession.

3 Quick reactions mentally, physically and tactically when possession immediately changes.

Figure 15

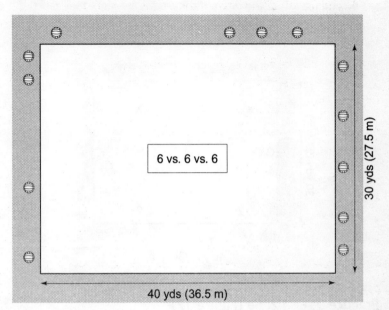

30 yds (27.5 m)

40 yds (36.5 m)

▓ What conditions could you impose upon Practices 6 and 7, and for what purpose?

Practice 8: The passing square (Figure 16)

Organization

1 4 vs. 4 with players on outside restricted to one or two touches who can't be tackled and must play the ball back inside the square within four seconds maximum.

2 4 vs. 4 situation in the square, but the players have always got an option of turning out and playing the ball off the players of the same team on the outside of the area. Play four minutes and change.

Key factors

1 Create space.

2 Quick play.

3 Look, play forward.

4 Regain possession.

Figure 16

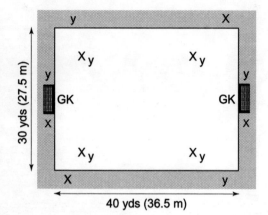

Practice 9: End zone (Figure 17)

Organization

1 8 vs. 8 or 9 vs. 9 plus two neutral players (possibly goalkeepers) supporting the team in possession.

2 Width of full pitch – penalty box to penalty box.

3 Team in possession has to run the ball over the 18 yards (16.5 m) line to score.

Key factors

1 Create space as a team.

2 Support the player in possession.

3 Pass and move.

Figure 17

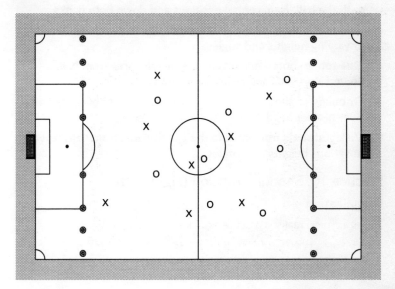

Shooting

Best Practice It is important that all players practise shooting, not just those who usually play in attacking positions. Certain situations are more likely to produce goals than others, and some goal-scoring situations occur more often than others. Consequently, more time needs to be spent on some techniques than on others.

The priority list for crossing and shooting, with the most important technique first, is:

1 One-touch shots from inside the penalty area from balls served at various angles on the ground.

2 Headed shots from crosses.

3 One-touch volley shots in the penalty area from balls served at varying heights and angles.

4   Shots taken from outside the penalty area while running forward with the ball, from central positions and down both flanks.

5   Two-touch shots from inside the penalty area with the service at varying heights and angles.

6   One-touch shots from outside the penalty area from balls served at various angles on the ground.

7   Dribbling or shooting past the goalkeeper, or lobbing the ball over his/her head, when clear of the defence.

8   Volleyed shots from outside the penalty area from balls served at various heights and angles.

Practice 10: Shooting rotation (Figure 18)

Organization

This is a typical realistic practice situation.

1   The area is 40 yards (36.5 m) by 30 yards (27.5 m), preferably with two portable goals.

Figure 18

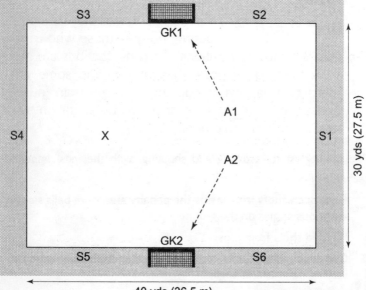

40 yds (36.5 m)

2 There are six servers, numbered 1 to 6 (S1–S6), each with a supply of four or five balls.

3 When the coach calls a server's number, they serve the ball for X to shoot. X must shoot alternately at GK1 and GK2, thus gaining practice in shooting from the left and from the right.

4 A1 and A2 are the support players.

5 When X shoots at the G1 goal, A1 attacks the goal.

6 The players rotate regularly so that each one in turn has concentrated practice in serving, shooting and supporting.

7 The goalkeepers, too, have sustained, concentrated, realistic practice.

Key factors

1 Take all opportunities to shoot.

2 Keep the ball low.

3 Follow in all shots.

Practice 11: One touch finishing (Figure 19)

This is a simple practice technique for when the ball is going away from the shooter.

Organization

1 Two players (O and X) face the goal.

2 Server (S) uses a number of service variations:

   a On the ground between the two players.

   b On the ground down the side of the players – biased towards one player or the other.

   c In the air over the players.

   d In the air down the side of the players.

3 Players compete as to who gets the one-touch finish in.

4 Either player competes for rebounds off the goalkeeper.

Statistic

Analysis tells us that approximately **70 per cent** of goals scored are with one-touch finishing.

Key factors

Specifically for the shooter

1   Needs to be bright and a quick thinker.
2   A quick mover – reactions.

Figure 19

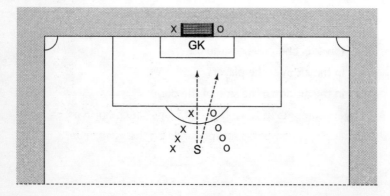

3 Be persistent – willing to keep missing.

4 Be brave – physically and mentally.

5 Be composed.

6 Needs a wide range of techniques.

Practice 12: 3 vs. 3 shooting (Figure 20)

Organization

1 Area of 30 yards (27.5 m) × 30 yards (27.5 m). Pitch divided by halfway line

2 3 vs. 3.

3 Goalkeeper starts by distributing the ball to either X1 or X2. Players can either shoot first time or combine with each other to get a shot on goal.

Figure 20

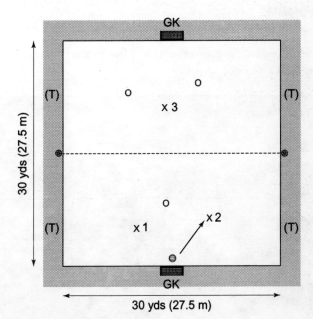

Key factors

1 Distribution.

2 First touch and body shape.

3 Take the first opportunity to shoot – when/where.

4 Shooting technique.

Progression/Variation

1 Two touch.

2 Goalkeeper can distribute to furthest player forward, i.e. goalkeeper can play to X3 who can either shoot or combine with X1/X2.

3 Introduce target players on the outside who are restricted to one or two touch to encourage more combination play.

Practice 13: 5 vs. 5 shooting (Figure 21)

Organization

1 Area of 40 yards (36.5 m) × 40 yards (36.5 m); two goals.

2 6 vs. 6 (including goalkeepers) and five target (T) players on outside.

3 Goalkeeper distributes the ball to any of their players. Can players get a shot on target or can they pass with target players to create a shooting opportunity?

4 Target players are limited to one or two touches.

5 The session will encourage quick play and combination play in and around the box.

Key factors

1 Goalkeeper's distribution.

2 First touch and body shape.

3 Take opportunities to shoot.

4 Shooting technique.

5 Angles of support.

Figure 21

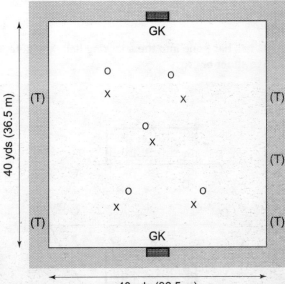

Practice 14: Diamond shooting (Figure 22)

Organization

1 Six balls in each net.

2 4 vs. 2 in each half.

3 Players must shoot from their own half initially, with the two forwards following in for rebounds.

4 Goalkeepers can only throw into their own half.

5 Any shots over the bar, the shooter is substituted by one of the fielders.

6 Defenders play two touch.

Key factors

1 Take the first shooting opportunity.

2 Accuracy before power.

3 Follow shots in for rebounds and secondary chances.

Development

1 Once the ball has gone into the attacking half, any defender can go wide to shoot or cross.

Figure 22

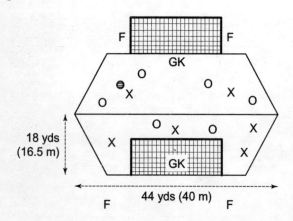

2 When the ball enters the attacking half, any one defender can enter the attacking half to join in combination play.

3 When possession is lost, regroup back to 4 vs. 2.

What aspects of goalkeeping can you highlight for your goalkeepers in Practice 14?

Practice 15: Finishing from different angles (Figure 23)

Organization

1 Servers cross balls into the box (can be rolling ball or stationary ball) in order S1, S2, S3, S4.

2 Attackers (X) go individually or in pairs and must score first time. Particularly good for headers – but can be volleys, half-volleys, etc.

3 To progress the practice, passive defenders and active defenders can be introduced.

Key factors

1 The cross must eliminate the goalkeeper.

2 Cross the ball into space (not at attacker).

Figure 23

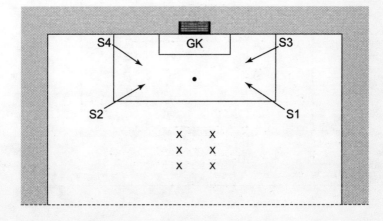

3 Timing and angle of run of the attacker.

4 Contact and finish by attackers.

▓▓ How would you make Practice 15 easier or more difficult for your players? How would you amend the reorganization using the NEAT formula?

Practice 16: Quick break and scoring from crosses (Figure 24)

Organization

1 Full pitch – but an area of 44 yards (40 m) by 35 yards (32 m) marked around the halfway line as shown in Figure 24.

2 Two wingers for each team in the flank channels.

3 Two groups of 4 vs. 4 in mid-field area and one neutral player (N) who plays for the team in possession.

Figure 24

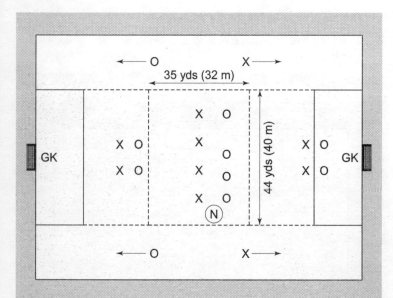

4   Two strikers opposed by two defenders, in each central end zone, and two goalkeepers.

Practice

1   The coach feeds a ball into one of the mid-field teams of four. They retain the ball for at least five passes using the floater if needed against the other mid-field group. On scoring five passes, they pass the ball forward to the foremost striker if possible, who is quickly supported by the deeper striker. The ball is then transferred to a winger who crosses the ball to the 2 vs. 2 situation in the box *and* one mid-field player who may break forward to get into a scoring position.

2   Should the defending mid-field team gain possession of the ball, they do not need to score five passes. They play the ball early to their strikers and one mid-field player may break into a scoring position to attack the cross from the winger.

Key factors

1   Playing the ball wide early.

2   Crossing the ball into dangerous areas.

3   Attacking the ball with diagonal runs.

4   Heading down.

■   How can you use Practice 16 to highlight defending aspects to work on? Would you need to change the organization and if so, how?

Statistic

At the highest level, the number of shots on target needed to score a goal is **3.4**.

Summary

- **This chapter has given 16 simple enjoyable practices to use with your squad of players to highlight attacking aspects.**

- **The practices can also be used to highlight defending issues.**

- **Planning is essential in order to achieve the maximum results from your coaching.**

- **Observe the activity and attitude of the players to make sure the practice is achieving the required purpose.**

- **Decide on the most appropriate three or four practices that you feel work well for your players and stick with them.**

- **Players like enjoyable practices that are familiar to them.**

- **The best coaches have a few well-tuned practices that meet the needs of their players.**

Self testers

1 Who should work hardest during a practice, the coach or the players?

2 List simple ways that you can progress a practice.

3 How can you 'condition' a game and for what reason?

Action plan

The practices shown in this chapter are tried and tested. Look over the ones you are not familiar with and try out five or six of them with your players over the course of a season. Don't try to experiment with all 16 of them in one season! Over a period of three seasons, settle upon your favourite five practices for passing and favourite five practices for shooting and crossing.

The FA

Chapter 5

LEARNING

Squad defending practices

THIS CHAPTER WILL:
- Provide practical advice on how to organize practices/
  games to help your team defend.
- Provide key points for you to observe and question.
- Give ideas for practice preparation to develop your
  session and players.

Players often think that they need only to fulfil their position role in the squad, i.e. if you are a defender that is your main role. However, it is important that as soon as your side loses possession, all players can become potential defenders and keep concentrating. This chapter has ten practices for you to use with your team. Many of the practices outlined in Chapter 4 can be used for defending aspects, and the principles regarding the organization of practices outlined in Chapter 4 will also apply to this chapter.

Sometimes opponents will outnumber defenders and be able to place dangerous crosses into the penalty box and make intelligent runs off the ball. These aspects and eventualities will need to be recreated so that your players have practice in dealing with these situations.

Do not continue pressurizing practices for more than ten minutes without a break because they will require higher levels of power endurance. Injuries can often be avoided if defending practices are curtailed before the players become too fatigued.

Please ensure that the environment is safe for the players to practice – avoid loose footballs disrupting the practice. Make sure that players are wearing the appropriate footwear and shin guards.

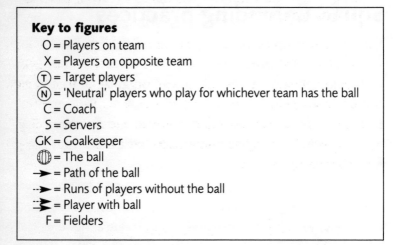

Key to figures

O = Players on team
X = Players on opposite team
(T) = Target players
(N) = 'Neutral' players who play for whichever team has the ball
C = Coach
S = Servers
GK = Goalkeeper
⬭ = The ball
➝ = Path of the ball
⇢ = Runs of players without the ball
⇒ = Player with ball
F = Fielders

Basic defending

Practice 1: 4 vs. 4 (Figure 25)

Organization

1 Practice takes place in a grid measuring 30 yards (27.5 m) by 20 yards (18 m), using full-sized portable goals.

2 There are four players, including a goalkeeper, on each side.

3 The players should be encouraged to shoot, if they have the space, as they can never be far from the opponent's goal. This

will also emphasize to the challenging players that they must be close enough to block the shot.

Key factors

1 Early decisions. The player nearest to the ball should always move to the challenge.
2 Clear communication. There should be clear communication between the players to establish who is to challenge the person with the ball. This should be followed up by the communication of information and encouragement from the covering player to the challenging player.

Sometimes there will be indecision as to which player is nearest to the player with the ball. In such circumstances there is a danger that either no player will challenge for the ball, or two players will challenge for the ball. Players will do well to remember that 'an early shout will sort it out'. Early calling, and talking to each other, is an important part of defending. It greatly assists in making early and correct decisions and in combining the skills of the defending players.

Figure 25

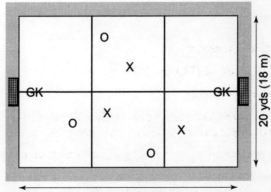

30 yds (27.5 m)

Practice 2: End-zone defending (Figure 26)

Organization

1 3 vs. 3.

2 The coach can pass the ball to either team.

3 He/she can vary the service to increase/decrease the time it takes the ball to reach the controlling player.

4 The controlling player must have two touches before he/she can release the ball.

5 Thereafter, free play.

6 As soon as the coach delivers the ball, defenders start defending.

7 To score, a team must get a player into the end zone with his/her foot on the ball by either a dribble, a run with the ball or a pass.

Key factors

1 Stopping opponents turning, where appropriate.

2 Forcing the player in possession wide wherever possible and appropriate by use of the defender's body angle.

Figure 26

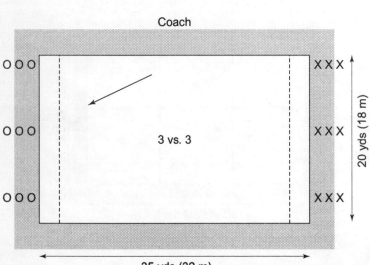

Practice 3: Inside or outside? (Figure 27)

Organization

1   3 vs. 3 plus two goalkeepers and two servers (servers play two touch).

2   Area of 30 yards (27.5 m) × 35 yards (32 m). Server's box is 10 yards (9 m) × 5 yards (4.5 m).

3   Start positions: GK X1 plays to X2 or X3.

Key factors

1   Marking space then pressure the ball with O3 and O4 when the ball is played wide.

2   Defenders decide to attempt to force play inside or outside.

3   Shape of three players observed at all times – O2, O3, O4.

4   Tracking runners.

5   Communication.

Figure 27

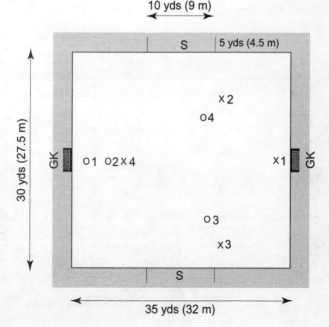

Practice 4: Defending 6 vs. 6 (Figure 28)

Organization

1 6 vs. 6 plus two goalkeepers and two servers who play on two touch when needed.

Figure 28

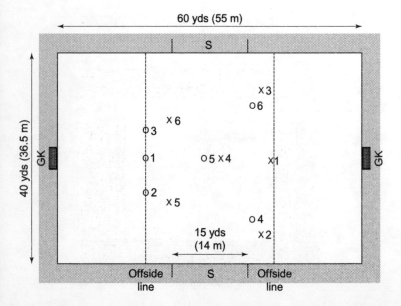

2   Area of 60 yards (55 m) × 40 yards (36.5 m). Server's area is 15 yards (14 m) long.

Key factors

As for 3 vs. 3 but to progress include:

1   Being compact.

2   Tracking runners.

3   Covering dangerous space.

Practice 5: 'Being compact' (Figure 29)

Organization

1   6 vs. 6.

2   Each team must have a forward who stays in the opponent's half.

3   Defending team must retreat to own half on losing possession.

4   Score by getting an attacking player in possession in one of the four end zones.

Key factors

1   Recover behind the ball as early as possible.

2   Shift across the pitch as a unit.

Figure 29

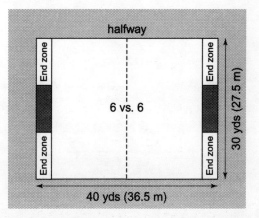

3   Tackle from the front.

4   Support the challenge.

Practice 6: 8 vs. 8 (Figure 30)

Organization

1   Game of 8 vs. 8 including goalkeeper on a pitch 70 yards
    (64 m) × 50 yards (46 m).

2   Footballs behind each goal.

3   Coach call a colour – yellow or red.

4   The goalkeeper of that colour team, who has a ball in their
    hand, can distribute the ball by hand to any of their players:

    a   in their own half of the field.

    b   as the game develops, anywhere in the field.

5   The game begins and continues until a shot at goal is taken or
    one minute elapses.

6   After one minute of play, or a shot at goal, players rest and
    recover for 30 seconds.

7   Coach calls out a colour to recommence the game.

Figure 30

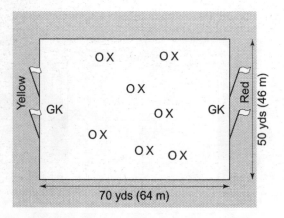

Key factors

Pressing – out of possession

1 Who presses the ball?

2 How – with what intention?

3 When does the press begin?

4 Reaction and responsibilities of other defenders to mark, track, cover, recover, etc.

◼ How could you condition this game to make it easier for the defenders to achieve their objectives?

Statistic

At the very highest level in a World Cup Final, possession changed from team to team on average every **15 seconds**.

Practice 7: 3 zones (Figure 31)

Organization

1 Three zones as indicated with five or six players in each zone (the larger the zone – more players).

2 Two goalkeepers who remain in one goal independent of team rotation.

3 Non-restricted touches.

4 Team 1 attacks Team 2, trying to score. Team 2 can press the ball in the free mid-zone. Therefore, play can be changed from here. When Team 2 wins the ball it must get the ball into the mid-zone. It can then regroup before attacking Team 3. If a goal is scored, then that team can continue to attack the next opponent.

5 If the ball is overhit into the free zone the ball is returned to the attacking team.

Figure 31

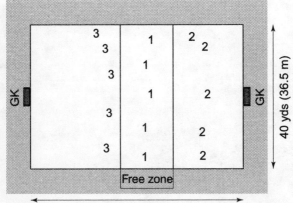

Quote

'League championships are usually won by the teams with the least number of goals conceded. It's the goals you don't concede that therefore win you the league.'

It's important that all players practice shooting and not just those that play in attacking positions.

Direct free kicks are potentially a very important factor in scoring goals and winning matches.

A team is most vulnerable when it has just failed an attack so always try to strike out of defence quickly.

Throw-ins occur more frequently than any other type of set play.

**Coaches should look to give verbal feedback that encourages players.
They should reward effort as well as attainment.**

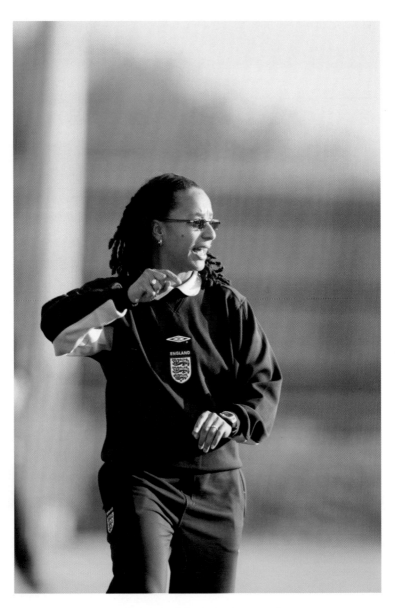

The qualities of a good coach include enthusiasm, patience, open mindedness, fairness and a willingness to help others improve.

Key factors

1 Remain compact.

2 Pressure the ball in groups.

3 Cover dangerous space.

Practice 8: 9 vs. 9 (Figure 32)

Organization

1 4 goals – 9 vs. 9.

2 Play one touch, two touches or free, as appropriate.

3 Play player-to-player marking or free, as appropriate.

4 No players are allowed in marked zones around goals: no goalkeepers.

5 To score: one team scores into the two goals joined together; the other team scores in two goals placed wide (change round at half-time).

Figure 32

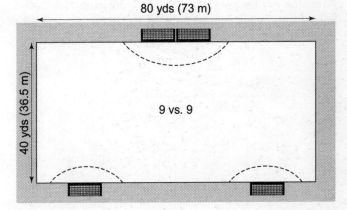

Key factors

As for 8 vs. 8 and include

1 Individual team strategies.

2 One team focus play inside.

3 One team focus play outside.

Practice 9: Pressing in opponent's half (Figure 33)

Organization

1 9 vs. 9.

2 Where practical, arrange teams in flexible 3-4-2 formation.

3 Goalkeepers must stay in the 'D' at the edge of the penalty area.

4 Goalkeeper can only distribute the ball into his/her defending half.

5 Offsides apply only behind dotted lines.

6 Score by passing the ball from anywhere on the pitch into the goalkeeper's hands.

7 When the goalkeeper catches the ball, the game is restarted immediately by him/her passing the ball in the defending half to the other team.

Figure 33

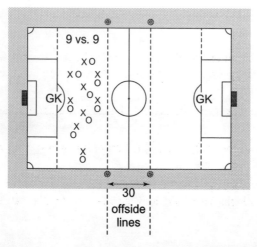

Key factors

1 All the previous aspects, especially concentration when attackers score.

2 They must defend immediately as the goalkeeper can now distribute the ball as quickly as he/she wants to opponents.

3 Pressurizing the opponent's half.

4 Angles and distances of pressurizing and supporting players.

Practice 10: Defending crosses (Figure 34)

Organization

1 A line of cones are placed 5.5 yards (5 m) in from the edge of the penalty area down the sides. Another line extends the sides of the box.

2 Wide attackers X2, X3, X7, X11 start in the zone outside these markers.

3 The back four O2, O5, O6, O3 mark up against X10, X9 in the central area.

4 A server, S plays a ball to the left-sided striker X10 who must pass to X3. X3 plays the ball into the zone beyond the markers. O2

Figure 34

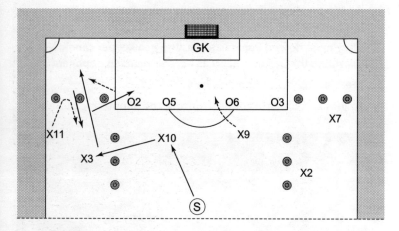

must put X11 under pressure as he/she retrieves the ball. X11 must now bring the ball back across the line of markers before crossing into the box for the run of X9 attempting to strike.

5 The practice is then repeated to the right.

Key factors

1 The movement of the back four up and down as a unit (i.e. adjusting to the movement of the ball and the pressurizing of O2).

2 Distance between the players (what is it they are defending?).

3 The positioning of the second defender (where does O5 go?).

4 The relationship with the goalkeeper (where does O6 go?).

5 Defending the far post (where does O3 go?).

Progression

1 Allow X11 to pass back over the cones to X3 who can deliver. The back four will now have to push up quicker.

2 Allow X3 to pass back to the server who can switch play to X2. The back four must now move up and across.

3 Increase the speed of the practice by allowing X3 to hit a diagonal to the other corner (i.e. X7).

Summary

- This chapter has given you ten simple enjoyable practices to use with your squad of players to highlight defensive aspects.

- Defending practices can sometimes resort to the repetition of pressuring the player on the ball.

- It is important to practice other aspects of defending – involving players further away from the ball.

- Please ensure that players wear the appropriate footwear and shin guards for the practices outlined.

Self testers

1 Is it more valuable to practice defending for full-size goals or five-a-side goals?

2 What is the minimum number for a team for realistic defensive squad practices?

3 What simple targets can you provide for the defending team when they gain possession of the ball?

Action plan

1 Look back over your team's last ten games and review the goals you have conceded in open play.

2 Which of the following scenarios describes the goals conceded:

- Lack of pressure on the ball?

- Insufficient support from the pressurizing player?

- Not tracking runners?

- Poor marking positions?

- Inability to cover dangerous space?

- Failure to defend crosses?

3 Can you find practices amongst the ten in this chapter to use to address these weaknesses?

Chapter 6

![bar]

Attacking set plays

> THIS CHAPTER WILL:
> - Help to identify key ways of achieving more set plays.
> - Look at why set plays are important.
> - Explore different set play permutations.
> - Assist in the understanding of the key factors in successful set plays.

Set plays are understood to be those occasions when the game needs to be restarted from corners, free kicks, throw-ins and penalties. Set plays have always been a major factor in winning soccer matches. The more important the match and the closer the contest, the more likely it is that the match will be decided by a set play. Thirty-three goals were scored in the World Cup Finals between 1966 and 2002. Of these, 16 came from moves started by set plays and five more when the ball was regained immediately following a set play.

Statistic

In the World Cup 2002 in Korea and Japan, almost **half of all goals** came directly or indirectly from a set play (a total of **78** goals including penalties). The overall proportion of goals from set plays was very similar to that reported for Euro 2000.

Why set plays are such an important source of goals

There are four major reasons why set plays are an important source of goals:

1 A dead ball.
2 Lack of pressure.
3 Extra attacking players.
4 Rehearsal.

A dead ball

The ball is still and on the ground or, in the case of a throw-in, safe in the thrower's hand. A still ball is much easier to play than one which is moving.

Lack of pressure

Defending players must be at least 10 yards (9 m) from the ball at corners and free kicks, making it difficult to disturb the kicker or put on the kind of pressure that causes inaccuracy. This does not apply to throw-ins, but there the thrower has the considerable advantage of using his/her hands.

Extra attacking players

At set plays, teams can put seven or eight players in attacking positions, something that never happens in the normal course of play. Having so many players forward makes it more difficult for the defenders to clear the ball, which is why so many goals come from regained possessions following set plays.

The advantage does not come simply from weight of numbers. A set play allows players to take up positions that suit their individual strengths, tall central defenders can get into position to head for goal, for example, while one or two good volleyers of the ball take up positions to return half-clearances.

Rehearsal

The more that teams practise and rehearse their set moves, the more accurate and well-coordinated their performance will become. The more accurate and well-coordinated their performance, the more successful a team will be, and with success comes more confidence. First, however, comes practice.

Players can be positioned for all eventualities. For instance, a back-header from a near-post corner might go into the goal, but it might also be flicked into the mid-goal area or to the far post, and players should be positioned to take these chances.

There is a further benefit from rehearsing moves. It helps players to develop their concentration. It is not enough for players to know what they should be doing. They must concentrate in order to do it effectively and to do it whenever required. Players who lose concentration tend to drift out of the game.

Ways to gain more set plays

Teams do not generally set out with the aim of gaining set plays. Set plays come as a by-product of positive play which puts pressure on opponents. For instance, a corner may result from a deflected shot at goal, or a free kick from a beaten defender's challenge. Set plays are second prizes when quality play has failed to succeed.

There are five things an attacking team can do that make it likely that defenders will concede a set play – either a throw-in, corner kick or a free kick of some kind:

1 Passing to the back of the defence.
2 Crossing to the back of the defence.
3 Dribbling.
4 Pressuring defenders.
5 Shooting.

1 Passing to the back of the defence

Passing behind defenders will cause problems. If the ball is played past a defender, they will be in the uncomfortable position of having to turn and run towards his/her own goal. They either have to attempt to turn and play back to the goalkeeper, which is very risky unless there is plenty of space, or play the ball out for a throw-in or a corner.

If in doubt, good defenders will always play the ball dead. Safety first is the golden rule in the defending third.

2 Crossing to the back of the defence

Crosses behind defenders, especially into prime target areas, cause defenders maximum discomfort. Most of them, running back towards their own goal, will settle for putting the ball behind for a corner kick.

Players attacking down the wings sometimes dwell on the ball, trying to find more space for a cross, then end up passing the ball back to a supporting player. Most of the time they would do better to take a chance and try to get the cross in early. If they succeed, the ball will get to the back of the defence. If they fail, quite often it is because the cross is knocked away by a defender for a throw-in or a corner.

3 Dribbling

Most defenders would consider they had won a duel with a dribbler if they had put the ball out for a corner or a throw. In fact, if a set play results from a dribble, the attacker, not the defender, has come out on

top. A set play, particularly in the attacking third of the field, is a perfectly acceptable result from a dribble, and another good reason for more players to dribble more frequently in attack. More goals are scored, directly and indirectly, from free kicks than from corners and throw-ins combined.

Dribbling is an important part of the game in the attacking third, and most teams could boost their goals tally simply by dribbling more in advanced positions.

4 Pressuring defenders

Pressure is exerted on a player in possession of the ball by challenging or moving forward, cutting down on the time and space available in which to play. If a defender is first to the ball when it is played to the back of the defence, an attacker should challenge as soon as possible. When time and space are limited, high demands are put on technique, and defenders who are not confident about their technique will frequently panic. When this happens, the ball can go anywhere. If a defender has once been forced into a position like this in a match he/she will start to worry about it happening again – leading to more uncertainty and panic.

Any tactic which discomfits defenders and encourages them to panic is useful to an attacking side in increasing the number of set plays they are awarded. Making sure that defenders on the ball are continually put under pressure certainly comes into this category.

■　Analyse your own team for three games and assess how your team gains its throws, free kicks and corner kicks.

5 Shooting

Quick and early forward play increases the number of shooting opportunities, and the more shots a team has, the more likely it is to score. The more often a team shoots, the more secondary shooting opportunities it creates.

Some of these come from rebounds and others from corners, either because the shot hits a defender or because the goalkeeper pushes it wide or over the bar. Teams that are prepared to shoot at every opportunity are difficult to defend against. Defenders are under extra pressure not to allow the attackers a sight of goal and are therefore more likely to make a mistake or give away a set play.

Applying these five positive principles will increase the number of set plays a team is awarded in a game. This is not to say that a team should go out looking for set plays, simply that quick early forward play and a positive approach will produce more set plays as a matter of course. With set plays involved in nearly half of all goals scored, more set plays can only mean more goals.

Direct free kicks

Direct free kicks are potentially a very important factor in scoring goals and winning matches. Sometimes free kicks present a good chance of scoring with a direct shot. The simpler the play, the greater the chance of success. At other times, there is very little chance of scoring direct, and the aim of the kicker should be to set up a chance of a goal for a teammate.

Wider free kicks

The wider the angle from which a free kick is taken, the more important it is to do two things; play the ball to the back of the defence and challenge the free defending players.

Defenders dread balls played in behind them, but if a free kick is accurately taken they are powerless to stop it. Ideally the ball should be played with inswing and spin toward the near half of the goal (this means a left-footed kick from the right flank or a right-footed kick from the left flank). This forces the defenders to turn and try to deal with a ball which is spinning and swerving away from them.

Figure 35

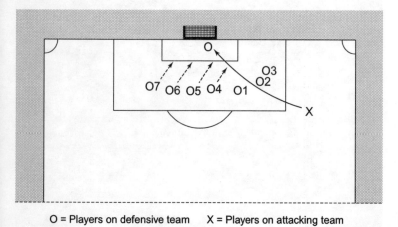

O = Players on defensive team　　　X = Players on attacking team

If the goalkeeper takes responsibility for setting the defensive wall at a free kick, the defenders' attention is often distracted. Quick-thinking attackers can exploit this to score.

In Figure 35, X has played the ball with inswing past the two-player wall and over the head of the other players who have to turn and attempt to clear a ball which is swinging away from them. To make their job even more difficult, each of the defenders should be challenged by an attacker.

In Figure 36, X is positioned for a free kick just outside the corner of the penalty area. From this position, a defending team would normally erect a wall with two, or possibly three, players in it.

The most vulnerable space in these circumstances is in the area near the post. There is nothing defenders can do to stop the ball being played into that area. Should a defender move in line with the ball and the front half of the goal, the ball can still be played round or over the player. Given an accurate delivery, problems are posed. The kick from the right is best

Figure 36

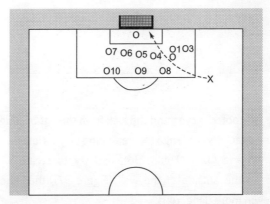

Figure 37

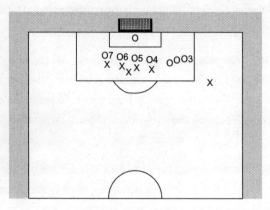

Figure 38

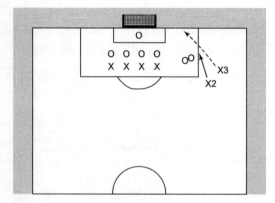

taken by a left-footed player, and the kick from the left by a right-footed player. If the attackers challenge the defending players level with the wall (O4, O5, O6 and O7 in Figure 36), and try to create a numerical advantage on the outside of the wall (Figure 37), then the situation becomes even more dangerous.

Given the accuracy of the kick, and the determination of the X players to be first to the ball, the situation for the O players becomes difficult.

Sometimes defenders do not defend the space on the outside of the wall, the space occupied by O3 in Figure 37. Two players should position to take the kick. If the space outside the wall is not defended (as in Figure 38), then one of the X players should attack the space and receive the ball behind defenders. X2's main concern now, before he/she delivers the ball, is to check the position of the goalkeeper.

The attacking team should not send too many players in to attack behind defenders. Two attacking players should be positioned on the edge of the penalty area (Figure 39) to deal with partial clearances. They will also be in a good position to counter any possible threat of a quick breakaway.

There are three key factors that contribute to successful free kicks from wide angles around the penalty area:

Figure 39

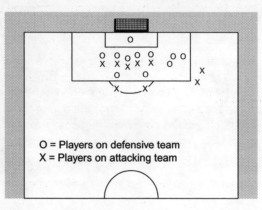

O = Players on defensive team
X = Players on attacking team

1 Simplicity and organization.

2 Accuracy of delivery.

3 Determined attacking players challenging opponents in the area
   inside the wall and to the first ball.

▇▇▇ A scatter graph of free kicks given in the attacking third
of the field reveals that a very high percentage are awarded
in flank positions. Devote time to practise free kicks from
these areas.

Progression

Organization

This practice must take place on a pitch in the attacking third of the field.

There are six phases to the practice:

1 The defenders get into position as shown in Figure 36 and X
   practises hitting the target area in the front half of the goal. X
   will only need to establish accuracy.

2 Five attacking players are brought in to challenge the defending
   players on the inside of the wall, and a second X player is

positioned in the area of the ball, as in Figure 37. The position of O3 must be varied to provide practice in attacking the space outside the wall in addition to attacking the space in the front half of the goal.

3   Once the players are comfortable and are achieving success in the previous phase, the practice should be expanded to include the remainder of the O and X players as in Figure 39. A competition should take place, involving five or ten kicks, from various positions on the corner of the penalty area and out towards the touchline.

4   Repeat phase 1 but from the left-hand side of the penalty area.

5   Repeat phase 2 from the left-hand side of the penalty area.

6   Repeat phase 3 from the left-hand side of the penalty area.

Key factors

1   Observe the accuracy of the kick into the front half of the goal.

2   Observe the ability of the two attackers on the ball to exploit space to the outside of the wall.

3   Observe the ability of the attackers to challenge defenders inside the wall, get close to their opponents, and then move away to be first to the ball.

4   Observe the ability and determination of the attacking players to attack the ball.

5   Observe the percentage success of the attacking players.

▓▓▓   Double-check that you have allocated the appropriate players for their most suitable job.

Direct free kicks from central positions

The goalkeeper will usually be in a position slightly off centre of his/her goal so that he/she can see the ball and protect the goal from a chip over the defensive wall, or a driven shot onto the part of the goal not protected by the defensive wall. Attacking tactics, therefore, should be based on obscuring the goalkeeper's view of the ball in order to slow down their reaction to any shot – driven or chipped.

Obscuring the goalkeeper's view

This tactic is easily achieved by using two attackers to complete the defensive wall, blocking the whole of the goal. In Figure 40, the two X players are used to complete the defensive wall. They are positioned less than 10 yards (9 m) from the ball for two reasons:

1   If they were more than 10 yards (9 m) away from the ball and beyond the defensive players they would be offside.

2   By moving to a position 6–7 yards (5.5–6.5 m) from the ball, they block more of the goal than they would at 9 yards (8 m).

They could, of course, position 1–2 yards (0.9–1.8 m) from the ball. This would have advantages in terms of blocking the goal and the goalkeeper's view. However, the players would be too far away from the goal to have a reasonable chance of attacking the goal, after the shot, to score from the rebounds from the goal structure or the goalkeeper.

Figure 40

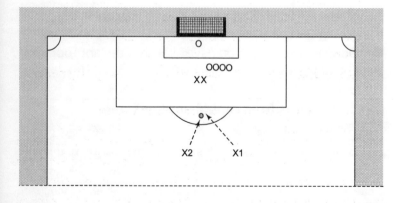

Therefore, 6–7 yards (5.5–6.5 m) distant from the ball, achieves the dual objectives of:

- Blocking the goalkeeper's view.
- Attacking the goal for rebounds.

It is important that the two attackers should work together:

- They should stand close together with their feet also close together. If this position is not adopted the goalkeeper will gain sight of the ball.
- They should break after the ball has been kicked. It is essential to keep watching the ball until the ball has been kicked. If they break early then the goalkeeper will gain sight of the ball.
- When they break, the outside player should spin to his/her right and the inside player should spin to his/her left. Both players should converge on the goal and attack the ball if there is a rebound.

Taking the kick

Two players should position to take the kick. There are four reasons for this:

1 The opposition will be in doubt as to which player is going to strike the ball.

2 The two players approach the ball at speed from different angles, so making different types of kick possible. It is even better if one of the players is right-footed and the other left-footed.

3 By approaching the ball at different angles, decoy play is much easier.

4 The player not striking the ball can act as a screen.

The two players will have decided from their assessment of the situation which type of kick has the best chance of scoring, and which one of them is best equipped to take the kick. The decision may be made that one player will make the run slightly earlier than the other to act as a decoy

Figure 41

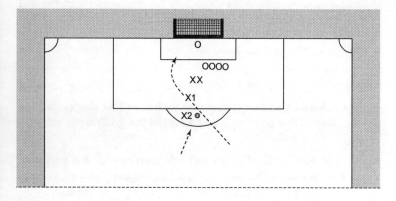

for the second player to strike the ball. If this is the case, then the player running as a decoy should run slightly in front of the ball, rather than over the ball, in order to act as a screen for the player striking the ball (see Figure 41).

As the ball is hit, X1 should be outside the line of the goal but bending his/her run to attack the goal for possible rebounds (Figure 41).

X1 and X2 should practise synchronizing their runs. A good understanding between the two players involved in the kick and the two players completing the wall is important. This understanding should be based on the following:

- The attacking players in the wall will stand firm for the player making the first run in order to block the goalkeeper's view of the kick. This does not necessarily mean that the player making the first run will not play the ball. It does mean that he/she will not attempt to drive the ball through his/her own wall.

- **The attacking players in the wall will always break for the second player taking the kick, but will continue to watch the ball as they turn to attack the goal for rebounds.**

Defending teams may withdraw all 11 players to defend against free kicks in the 'D'. Attacking teams could afford to send nine players forward, including the kicker. Attacking players should position themselves close to each defending player who is marking space to the side of the wall. Defenders do not like being treated in this way and they usually defend less well under such physical and mental pressure.

In Figure 42, all the O players to the side of the wall are marked by the attacking X players. O7 and O8 are not marked because they are positioned to threaten the kick. X4 is positioned behind the two X players involved in the kick and will move forward into the 'D', as the kick is taken, to deal with any ball cleared to the edge of the penalty area. All the other X players, including the kicker, should concentrate on attacking the 6-yard (5.5-m) area after the kick is taken.

Figure 42

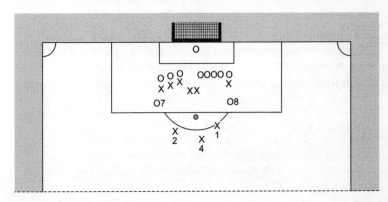

▓   Rehearse set plays on a regular basis and if the selected players know their responsibilities, you can interrupt squad practices, five-a-side games or fitness work for set play practice.

Progression

Organization

This practice should take place on a pitch using a penalty area. There are four phases to the practice:

1 The organization is as in Figure 40. The goalkeeper, plus the defensive wall of four players, should be placed in position. Two attacking players should position to block the goalkeeper's view of the ball and two further attacking players should position to take the kick. The players should practise four basic shots:

   • Chip shot over the defensive wall.

   • Chip shot over the attackers' wall.

   • Swerve shot round the outside of the attacker's wall.

   • Drive through the attackers' wall

   Once the attacking players have linked their movements and combined, the practice should be developed.

2 The organization is as in Figure 42. The remainder of the defence is brought into the practice and the players are allowed to position where they please. Five further attackers are introduced. Four occupy defenders to the side of the wall and one defender is positioned just outside the 'D'. Practice of each of the four types of shot taken in the previous phase then takes place.

3 Once the attacking players are comfortable in their performance, a competition of five or ten shots from various positions inside the 'D' would be very productive.

4 Free play 11 vs. 11 interspersed with wide and central free kicks.

Key factors

1 The two attacking players completing the defensive wall should do the following:

   a Position less than 10 yards (9 m) from the ball.

   b Block the goalkeeper's view of the ball.

   c Attack the goal for rebounds after the kick has been taken.

2 The two players involved in the kick should do the following:

   a Approach the ball from different angles.

   b Produce effective decoy movements.

   c Produce an effective screen if the second player is striking the ball.

   d Make a direct shot at goal.

3 The two attacking players in the wall should co-ordinate with the two players involved with the taking of the kick.

4 The attacking players should mark the defending players marking space to the side of the wall. They should attack the 6-yard (5.5-m) area once the kick is taken.

5 One attacking player should remain in the 'D' to deal with a ball which is partially cleared.

6 Observe the percentage success of the various types of shots.

Indirect free kicks

Free kicks inside or around the 'D'

A direct shot must be made on the second touch by a second player for an indirect free kick, i.e. the first player cannot play the ball twice. A slight adjustment in the positioning of the attacking wall is the main requirement.

In Figure 43, X1 will make a short pass for X2 to shoot. X3 and X4, a couple of metres away from the ball, are blocking the goalkeeper's view. They must break as late as possible, leaving the goalkeeper as little time as possible to see the ball.

Figure 43

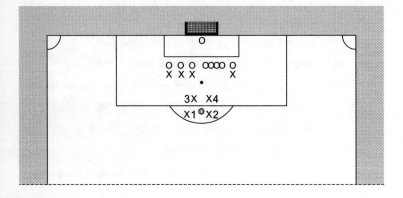

Whether the ball is played slightly to the right or to the left on the first touch will depend very much on how X1 and X2 see the situation and which angle to goal they wish to widen. For example, if X2 plays the ball a metre to the left, it will open up an angle to attack the area of goal to the goalkeeper's left. That could be particularly dangerous if X1 swerved the ball away from the goalkeeper with his/her left foot.

Best Practice alternative indirect free kick

In Figure 44:

- X1 rolls the ball to X2 who stops it for X3 to shoot.

- As X3 runs in, X2 drags the ball back, turning away from the defending player attempting to block the shot.

- X2 will now have a clear shot.

Free kicks inside the penalty area

These do not occur often but your team should be prepared. All 11 defending players withdraw into the penalty area. If the kick is within 10 yards (9 m) of the goal, then the probability is that all 11 will be on the

Figure 44

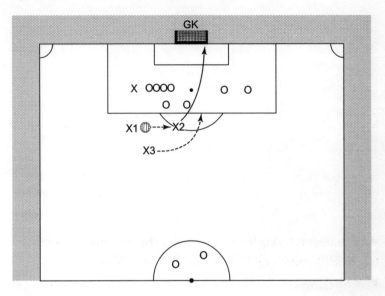

goal line between the posts. In such circumstances, the whole team will advance towards the ball in a block once the ball is in play and before the shot is taken. There are four important factors to consider:

1   If the kick is at a narrow angle then the first touch should widen the angle. In Figure 45, X1 has widened the angle for X2 to shoot through.

2   If the ball is less than 10 yards (9 m) from the goal, as is the case in Figure 45, the ball should be played backwards on the first touch to give the second player more time and more space for the shot.

3   It is important to observe the position of the goalkeeper and direct the shot over the heads of defenders in the area where the goalkeeper is not positioned.

Figure 45

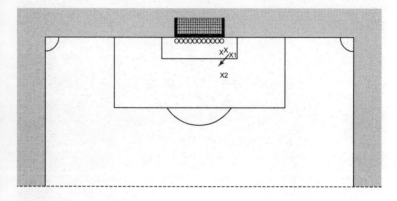

4   The players taking the kick should try hard to remain calm in a situation which often lends itself to utter confusion.

Progression

Organization

This practice should take place in the penalty area on a pitch and should, ideally, form part of a concentrated session on direct and indirect free kicks.

Key factors

1   The two players in the attackers' wall should adjust their position so that they are a couple of metres from the ball. They should break as late as possible.

2   The players taking the kick should assess the situation and attack the most vulnerable area of the goal, widening the angle of the kick if necessary.

3   If the kick is less than 10 yards (9 m) from the goal, they should give themselves more time and space by playing the ball backwards for the shot.

4   Observe the accuracy of the execution.

5   The players involved in the kick should remain calm.

▨ If you were England manager how would you organize the team to attack at free kicks?

Throw-ins

Players seem to relax their concentration more at throw-ins than at any other time. They are a possible route to winning a goal. There are six key things to remember to make throw-ins an attacking move:

1 Take the throw quickly.
2 Throw to an unmarked player.
3 Throw forward.
4 Throw for ease of control.
5 Create enough space for the throw to be effective.
6 Get the thrower back into the game.

Take the throw quickly

If defending players' concentration lapses – as it often does when the ball goes out of play – this should be exposed immediately. The throw

must be taken as quickly as possible, which means that the person nearest the ball should take the throw.

The only exception to this rule is for a long throw in the attacking third of the field (see page 154), when time needs to be taken for extra players to move forward into attacking positions and the ball given to the long throw specialist.

Throw to an unmarked player

An unmarked attacking player should be able to initiate forward play faster than any other; they are the best player to receive the ball.

Throw forward

In the attacking third of the field, the ball should always go forward if possible, and preferably to a player who can turn with the ball. If the player who is to receive the ball is marked, they should always be supported.

Throw for ease of control

A throw-in is a pass. The ball should be delivered with the same consideration as a pass, and thrown at a pace, and an angle, which makes it as easy as possible for the receiver to bring it under control and as difficult as possible for any defender to challenge it.

If the thrower wants the ball headed back to them, they should aim to deliver it chest high. This will make it easy for the receiver to move towards the ball and head it through its top half, directing it down to the feet of the thrower.

Figure 46

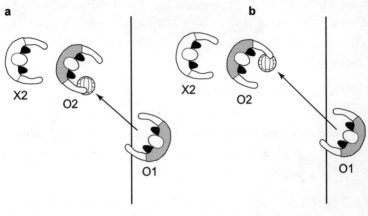

In **a**, O1 has thrown the ball to the right foot of O2. This makes it difficult for O2 to screen the ball from X2.

O2's task is made easier, and X2's more difficult, if O1 throws the ball to O2's left foot, as in **b**.

Create enough space for the throw to be effective

Players often make a mistake in standing too close to the thrower. In fact, they should spread out at a throw-in. This makes it more difficult for defenders to mark them and to cover each other and it creates space to exploit.

In Figure 47, O2 and O3 have both made runs toward O1. Their markers have followed them. Space has, as a result, been created behind X3, into which O1 can throw the ball for O4 to run on to. O4 will be marked by X4, but X4 will be in a one against one situation with no cover.

The pause in play at a throw-in makes it easy for attackers to move about and interchange positions. Since defenders have to react instantly to pre-planned and rehearsed moves, it becomes extremely difficult for them to mark and cover effectively.

Figure 47

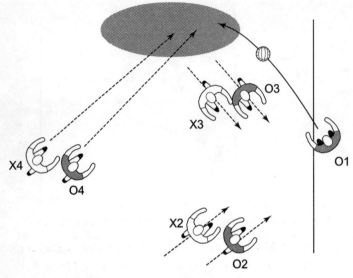

O = Players on team   X = Players on opposite team

Long throw-ins in the attacking third

The most effective long throw is fast and at head height to the area of the near post. An attacker who is tall and a good header of the ball should take up position here to flick the ball into the mid-goal area or to the far post. The rest of the team should be positioned in support across the whole penalty area, ready to attack the ball when it is flicked on or to challenge for any partial clearances.

Without organized team support, long throws rarely achieve anything. With that support, and a good throw, the defenders have considerable problems and goals will inevitably come.

Get the thrower back into the game

The player taking the throw-in should not think their task is finished once they have delivered the ball. If the player they have thrown to is marked,

Figure 48

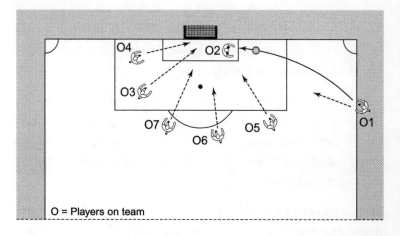

the thrower should move towards them to give support. At the very least the thrower should provide an extra player in the area of the ball.

In Figure 48, O1 has thrown the ball to O2. O3 is positioned to attack the mid-goal area and O4 the far post. O5, O6 and O7 are in support positions ready to challenge for half-clearances. Note that O1 follows their throw into the area to support O2 and pick up on half-clearances in that area. All the attacking players should delay their runs forward to the last possible moment in order to make it as difficult as possible for the defenders to mark them.

Defending teams sometimes position someone near the thrower to stop the ball being played back to them. This marker may well feel their job is done if the ball is not played straight back to the thrower, who should put them to the test by joining in the attack once the throw has been taken.

Penalty kicks

The importance of penalty taking has increased in recent years, with penalty 'shoot-outs' now widely used to decide matches in cup competitions. Consequently, all players, and not just one or two specialists, should practise taking penalty kicks.

Successful penalties come as a result of the combination of the right temperament and the right technique. The ideal penalty taker should have a calm, even temperament. They should be able to shut out everything around them and concentrate on a confident, positive technical performance.

There are basically two techniques for taking penalties: placement and power. Placement kickers use a side-footed technique to stroke a shot along the ground just inside a post; power kickers attempt to beat a goalkeeper with the simple force and speed of their shot. Whatever the choice, penalty takers should make up their minds about what they are going to do and stick to it. Nothing is worse in a penalty taker than indecision. If the goalkeeper anticipates correctly and the ball lacks pace, then the shot is saved. The best technique is to aim for either of the corners and hit the ball accurately with pace. All attacking players should attack the ball for rebounds.

As the penalty taker strikes the ball, their teammates should be beginning their runs into the area for possible rebounds. Realistic penalty practices should include these other outfield players as well as the penalty taker and a goalkeeper, as the timing of these runs into the area is crucial; moving too soon is illegal, moving too late means the ball is more likely to be cleared.

Always remember that if the ball comes back off the bar or either post without the goalkeeper touching it, then the player who took the penalty

Figure 49

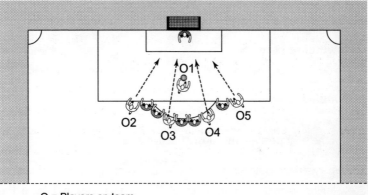

O = Players on team

must not play it. The kicker should follow in their shot, and four players – O2, O3, O4 and O5 – in Figure 49 should converge on the goal for possible rebounds, being sure not to stray inside the area until the kick has been taken.

Corner kicks

Through not as important as free kicks, corners are a prolific source of goals. There are two basic types of corner, short and long.

Short corners

The purpose of playing the ball short at a corner is to produce a numerical advantage of two against one, or three against two in the area of the corner flag, taking advantage of the law which keeps defenders at least 10 yards (9 m) from the ball.

This advantage is then used to position your players closer to the goal and at a better angle. Players who move out to support the short kick should move back into the danger area once it is taken.

Long corners

There are two types of long corner, depending on which way the ball is swung into the penalty area – outswinging and inswinging corners.

Outswinging corners

These do produce goals but are less effective than inswinging deliveries.

Inswinging corners

These are by far the most effective. Inswinging corners directed to the area of the near post are the most effective of all.

Some players and coaches have a mania about variety. They think that an outswinging corner after a series of inswinging ones will have the advantage of containing an element of surprise. In fact, it will be more likely to provide an element of relief for the defenders.

If the team organization is good, there will be an element of variety, but it will be a variation on a theme, and the theme that pays the highest dividends is an inswinging corner to the near post. Perfecting this type of

corner and persisting with it will markedly increase the number of goals a team scores from corners and from regained possession immediately following a corner.

Attacking players should be carefully selected for the various roles required. The most important is the kicker, who must be able to guarantee an accurate service; 80 per cent or four accurate kicks in every five, is an acceptable rate. The kicker should regularly practise their delivery as well as participating in the equally important team practice.

It is up to the rest of the team to support the kick and get the maximum out of it. Four players are needed in the 6-yard (5.5-m) box. Their precise positions and functions are important.

In Figure 50, O2 is positioned at the near post for a corner from the right. O2's job is to move towards the ball and flick it on across the goal if it is low in flight. O2 must be tall and capable of performing well under pressure.

Figure 50

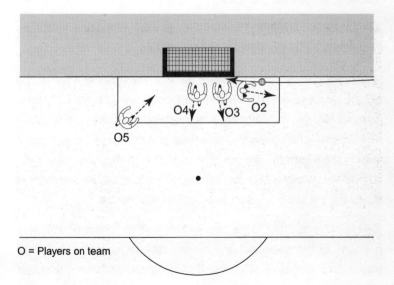

O = Players on team

O3 stands close to the goal line inside the near post. As the kick is taken, O3 moves out towards the edge of the 6-yard (5.5-m) box, where they can attack any ball entering the area below bar height. This may entail them moving out then in again. There are two reasons for this. By standing on goal line, both O3 and the player deputed to mark O3 will be obscuring the goalkeeper's view, and by moving in and out, O3 is more likely to create space for themselves than they would by standing still. O3 should also be tall and a good header of the ball. Sometimes they will head for the goal; often it will be better if they head across goal to the area of the far post.

The task of O4 is similar, but starts from the back half of the goal. Their move to the edge of the 6-yard (5.5-m) box when the corner is taken should allow them to watch the ball all the time; if it is flicked on they should be looking to attack it. The job of O5 is critical. They attack the area, by the far post. If the ball is flicked on by a teammate, or deflects off a defender, it is very likely to drop invitingly into the far-post area for a relatively simple scoring chance.

All four players should be careful not to be caught offside in the 6-yard (5.5-m) box if the corner kick is partially cleared.

Four more players should support the kick towards the edge of the penalty area. Figure 51 shows their positions for a right-side corner. O6 is on the far side of the penalty area, ready to attack the far post. O7 is near the edge of the penalty area, looking to attack the mid-goal area just outside the 6-yard (5.5-m) box. O8 and O9 hold their positions at the edge of the penalty area to pick up any rebounds or partial clearances. It is best if these two players are good volleyers of the ball.

Eight players and the kicker are shown here in advanced attacking positions, on the assumption that the opposition have pulled back all 11 players into defensive positions. If they choose to leave one player

Figure 51

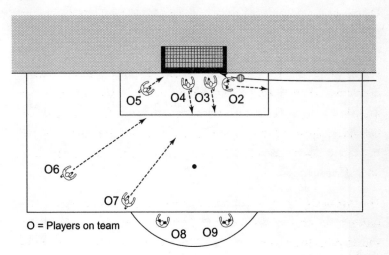

O = Players on team

upfield, then either O8 or O9 should go deeper, to the edge of the attacking third of the field.

Best practice alternatives for corners

In Figure 52:

* The dotted circles show where the players end up.
* They all start in these positions then, on the signal, jog out to the edge of the box.
* The target is C who starts the move with their curved run.
* D must get across the front of the keeper and the line of flight of the ball.
* E must attack the goalkeeper.
* F must lock in the far post.
* A and B will have attracted two defenders out to create space. Those remaining cannot defend the spaces in the 6-yard (5.5-m) box and mark the players effectively.

Figure 52

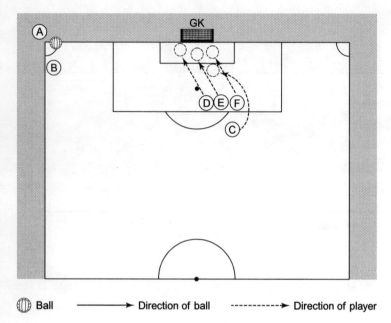

🏐 Ball   ⟶ Direction of ball   -------⟶ Direction of player

In Figure 53, there are two options:

Option A

- On a given signal, player C runs towards the ball down the goal line.
- Player D moves off the line.
- A plays the ball to C's feet and runs towards the box for a return pass.
- C shapes the pass but does a 'Cruyff' turn to find him/herself free on the edge of the 6-yard (5.5-m) box with a choice of D, E, F to pick out with a pass.

Option B

- Same movement, but A passes to B who sets the ball for A to deliver near post for D, or E to attack in the space vacated by C.

Figure 53

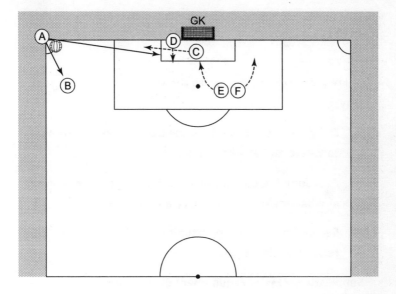

Practise set plays until the ball goes out of play as many goals from set plays originate from regained possession.

Summary

- There are recurring themes to the success of attacking set plays:

  - Delivery of the ball – how the ball is kicked or thrown, to where and at what pace.

  - Attacking the ball: arrangement of players – who runs, at what angles to which area and when to arrive.

  - Secondary scoring opportunities – rebounds and returns of clearances.

- Simplicity is a major requirement in the planning and execution of attacking set plays.

- For the factors outlined above to be consistently successful, planning and practice is crucial.

Self testers

1 Which of your players are the best at delivering crosses and free kicks?

2 Which of your players are good at quick headers?

3 Who in your team are the best and most aggressive headers of the ball?

4 Amongst your players, who is most likely to score from volleys or first-time shots outside the penalty area?

5 When does the set play finish?

Action plan

1   Over ten games check how many goals you have scored from set plays or regained possession from set plays. If this is below 50 per cent of all of your goals then you need to work on your team's set plays!

2   Give the players responsibility to decide – within an agreed plan – which players will perform the specific jobs.

3   Play a practice coached 11 vs. 11 game, with you as the coach and award your team numerous set plays for practice.

Chapter 7

Defending set plays

THIS CHAPTER WILL:
- Help you to defend free kicks.
- Develop ideas for defending throw-ins.
- Improve your management of corners.

Even the most confident and competent of teams will concede some set plays, of course. Set plays are difficult to defend against because the attacking team has three great advantages:

- **They can move a large number of players into pre-planned attacking positions.**
- **A player taking a kick cannot be pressured as defending players have to be 10 yards (9 m) from the ball.**
- **A player taking a kick or a throw has the advantage of a dead ball.**

The defence's problems may be deepened by two common mistakes:

- **The defence may not be properly organized to cope with the types of situations that arise during and after a set play.**

- Players' concentration may lapse because the game has stopped; sometimes, having moved into their assigned position, they feel the job is done and fail to concentrate on what they should be doing there.

Set plays often decide the result of the match, and this includes not only the set play itself but a possible secondary scoring chance immediately following it. Three qualities are needed for successful defending:

1 Planning and organization.
2 Individual and team discipline.
3 Concentration.

Planning and organization

Planning is necessary in order to make the opponents' job as difficult as possible both at the set play itself and if they regain possession following the set play. The aim is to get the best out of players as individuals and to combine their talents to produce the best possible team. Players must be carefully selected to fill specific positions.

Individual and team discipline

The efficiency of a team as a whole depends on each individual player thoroughly doing the job he/she has been given. This is true at all times, but particularly at set plays.

Concentration

Lapses in concentration are a major problem at set plays, yet concentration is vital if players are to successfully do the jobs they have been given.

Players must be given specific tasks and each situation should be rehearsed. They are then more likely to keep concentration, and the danger from set plays is reduced. Once the ball has been cleared the defenders should move up and out of the penalty area as quickly as possible in order to support the player with the ball and to play as many opponents as possible offside.

In tactical terms, the basic problem for the defending team at all set plays is to achieve the ultimate balance between marking players and marking space. It is not so much that one method is better than the other, simply that no team should rely on either method in isolation.

Free kicks in and around the penalty box

Direct free kicks near to the penalty area – setting a wall

When a free kick is conceded near to the penalty area, the defending team need to set up a wall to defend part of the goal. Unless a team is well organized and practised, when under pressure this can be disjointed. As a coach, check these four questions with your players:

1   Who positions the wall?
2   How many players in the wall?
3   How do the players in the wall line up?
4   When does the wall break?

Who positions the wall?

The job of setting the wall in position is often a combination of the goalkeeper and assigned player. The goalkeeper can set the wall and position themselves in line with a post and the ball while they satisfy themselves that the wall is in position (Figure 54). For a period of time however, if only for a few seconds, the whole goal is exposed. The task of the goalkeeper is to position themselves immediately to stop the major threat of the goal. That threat is the quick direct shot. The position of the goalkeeper must be:

- Where s/he can see the ball, not behind the defensive wall.
- Near to the centre of the goal.

Figure 54

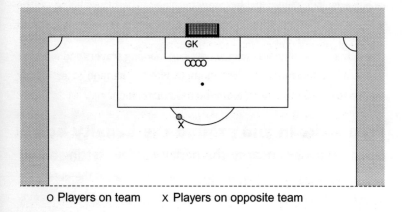

o Players on team   x Players on opposite team

Figure 55

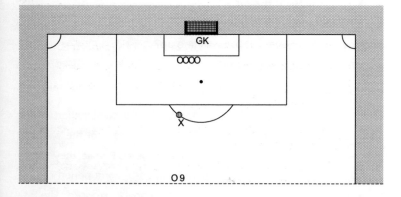

The out-field player nominated to set the wall should position themselves 10 yards (9 m) from the ball, behind the ball and in line with the post on which the wall is to be set (Figure 55). The choice of post must be predetermined. If the kick is at a wide angle, the wall should be set on the near post, thus greatly reducing the danger of the driven shot.

If the kick is in a central position, the choice should rest with the goalkeeper but should still be predetermined. The player lining up the wall, O9 in Figure 55, should only position one player. There is no need for O9 to attempt to position more than one player.

That player should be in a direct line between the ball and the post. They must also be 10 yards (9 m) from the ball. Once that player is lined up, it is vital that they do not move their position until after the kick is taken. While other players move to complete the wall, the player who has lined up the wall can assume other defensive duties.

How many players in the wall?

The answer to this question largely depends on the position of the ball. Do not place too many players in the wall because opponents in dangerous positions must also be marked. If, for example, six players were placed in the wall to defend against a central free kick in the 'D', there would be two disadvantages. First, the potential situation outside the wall would be eight attackers against four defenders. Second, the goalkeeper would have to move well across their goal, away from a central position, in order to see the ball. The answer to the question, therefore, lies in the following guide (Figure 56):

- If the kick is in a central position, in the 'D', the wall should contain four or five players.
- If the kick is between the 'D' and the corner of the penalty area, the wall should contain three or four players.
- If the kick is down the side of the penalty area, the wall should contain two or three players.

As the position of the kick goes out towards the touchlines, or out towards the edge of the defending third of the field, so the number of players in the wall should be reduced until finally just one player threatens the kick.

Figure 56

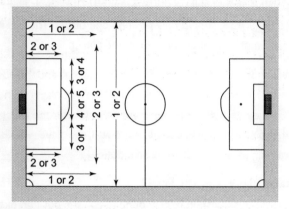

Teams should be organized in such a manner that they know exactly how many players are required in a wall in any given situation. The goalkeeper, however, can eliminate any possible confusion by shouting the number required.

How do the players in the wall line up?

Players should know exactly who goes into which wall, which two players on the right-hand side, which five in the central position, which three on the left and so on. It is also worth stressing that it is a mistake to lock up the best defending players in the wall.

Selecting players to go into the wall is simply an extension of your coaching to get the best out of the players as individuals and as a team. Once the players know who is going into the wall, and who will be lined up between ball and post, there are three factors to consider:

1   If there are three or more players in the wall, one of them should always be outside the player who is lined up; that is, outside the line between ball and post. The reason for this is to prevent the ball from being swerved round the outside of the wall and into the goal.

2   The players should position according to size so that the tallest
    is on the outside and the shortest is on the inside. The reason
    for this is that the tall players will block a greater part of the goal
    which is least accessible to the goalkeeper.

3   The players must position close together and their feet should
    also be close enough to prevent the ball from going between
    their legs.

It is also important that players in a wall should give themselves the
maximum possible protection. They can achieve this by crossing their
hands in front of their lower abdomen and slightly bowing their heads so
that the ball does not hit them directly in the face.

When does the wall break?

The wall should break once the kick is taken because it is unlikely that the
wall will remain at the correct angle. Breaking, however, does not mean
all the players moving off in different directions. On most occasions the
best advice is for the wall to move, en bloc, towards the ball.

As the attackers play the ball to the side to widen the angle for a shot at goal, so the defensive wall moves closer to the ball to narrow the angle. The quicker this is done, the more likely the defenders are to block the shot. Sometimes players in the wall link arms or hold each other around the waist. Try to avoid this so that:

- **The personal protection is good.**
- **The movement, after the kick is taken, is not restricted.**

It is vital that the wall is placed 10 yards (9 m) away from the ball. This is the law and there are considerable dangers if the wall is set 5 yards (4.5 m) away from the ball and then moved back by the referee. In Figure 57, it is clear that four players will seal off more of the goal at point A than at point B. At point B, a team would be extremely vulnerable to a direct shot. By placing the wall at point A, the goalkeeper will have to move farther across his/her goal to see the ball. This position makes him/her vulnerable to a ball chipped over the wall.

Figure 57

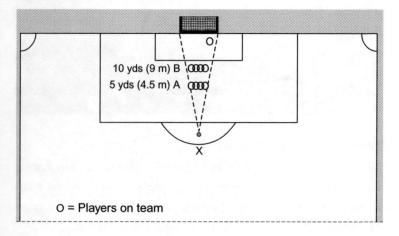

10 yds (9 m) B

5 yds (4.5 m) A

X

O = Players on team

Direct free kicks near to the penalty area – sealing off vital space

In defending against free kicks around the penalty area, withdraw all 11 players into defensive positions. How the players outside the wall are used is very important. The precise positioning of the players depends mainly on the positioning of the ball. There are two basic positions for the ball:

1 Free kicks in the D.
2 Between the 'D' and the corner of the penalty area.
3 Down the side of the penalty area.

Free kicks in the 'D' are the most dangerous of all. The area to seal off stretches from the edge of the six-yard box to the edge of the penalty area.

All ten defending outfield players are positioned to seal off space between the six-yard box and the edge of the penalty area. O2 is in line between the ball and the far post to block any shot aimed inside it. O3 and O4 may have to make slight adjustment in their positions to mark

Figure 58

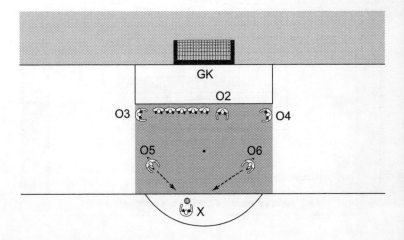

opponents but they should not be positioned outside the width of the six-yard box. They should be half-turned, so they can move quickly into the six-yard box to clear possible rebounds or blocked shots. O5 and O6 are positioned to threaten the kick, ready to move in to block the shot if the ball is played sideways for another player to shoot.

Free kicks between the 'D' and the corner of the penalty area
As the position of the kick moves to the side of the 'D', so the direct threat on goal decreases and the vital space to seal off increases. That space is about 32 yards (29 m) by 12 yards (11 m) as shaded (see Figure 59).

Figure 59 shows that there are only three players in the wall since the kick is near to the corner of the penalty area. The kick is threatened by one player, O9, from the inside. This is important because if the angle of the kick is changed, it is more dangerous on the inside than the outside.

O3 is positioned to meet the threat to the outside of the wall. As it is the left full-back's normal defensive position, he/she should be the best player in the team to defend that space. O4 is positioned in line between the ball and a point just inside the far post.

Figure 59

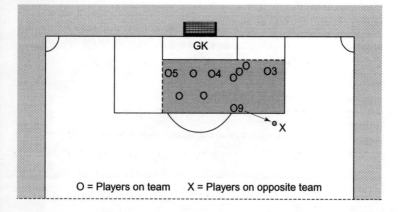

O5 is positioned outside the far post to deal with high crosses. It is important that this player is a good header of the ball. The position is usually best occupied by the centre-half.

Free kicks down the side of the penalty area

As the position of the ball is moved down the side of the penalty area, still more space has to be sealed off. In Figure 60, O3 still defends the space on the outside of the wall and O9 threatens the kick from a position square on the inside. The most critical position of all, however, is that of O4 who is defending the space in the area of the near post. The threat to the near post, particularly from an inswing kick, is great from all flank free kicks in positions just outside the penalty area. The threat remains from those taken even farther out.

Figure 60

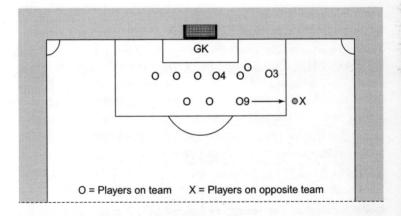

Indirect free kicks inside the penalty area

A direct shot is unlikely inside the penalty area, unless the kicker blasts the ball hoping for a ricochet into the goal. It is most likely that the angle of the ball will be changed and that the shot will come on the second touch – inter-passing movements will certainly not be in the minds of attacking players. If the ball is in a good shooting position, your defenders should:

- Cover as much of the goal as possible with a defensive wall. It could be, because of the 10-yard (9-m) law, that the wall will have to position on the goal line, with all 11 players between the posts. If this is the case, the goalkeeper should position in the centre of the wall.

- Once the kick is taken, and before the second touch is made, the wall should converge on the ball. This gives the best chance of smothering the shot and also gives an outside chance of catching opposing players offside.

Best Practice Practising set plays is time-consuming and involves little physical movement. Because of this, the players will get cold more easily than in a normal coaching session and may, if special care is not taken, become bored. Players should be comfortable and wear tracksuits.

▨ Adopt specific strategies to avoid conceding goals direct from set plays. Do you believe that by requiring the defensive wall to jump, it will reduce the chances of the opposition scoring with a direct shot? Avoid needless goals being scored from free kicks from rebounds from the goalkeeper not being cleared quickly enough or the opposition regaining possession in your team's penalty area.

Organization of the whole defence against free kicks

Practice in defending against free kicks around the penalty area takes place in six phases:

1a Organization of the whole defence against free kicks inside the 'D' without opposition.

1b Defending against free kicks in the 'D' with a full attack of nine players being given a free choice in selecting their positions.

1c After the necessary points and adjustments have been made a competition of five to ten free kicks, from inside the 'D', should be taken.

2a Organization of the whole defence against free kicks in the area from the edge of the 'D' to the corner of the penalty area, on the right-hand side, without opposition.

2b Defending in the above area against a full attack of nine players with a free choice of selecting their positions.

2c After the necessary points and adjustments have been made a competition of five or ten free kicks, inside the above area, should be taken.

3 As in point 2 but on the left-hand side.

4a Organization of the whole defence against free kicks in the area to the side of the penalty area, on the right-hand side, without opposition.

4b Defending in the above area against a full attack of nine players with a free choice of selecting their positions.

4c After the necessary points and adjustments have been made a competition of five or ten free kicks, inside the above area, should be taken.

5 As in point 4 but on the left-hand side.

6 A game is played in one half of the field. The coach blows the whistle at frequent intervals and places a ball in the position from which a free kick must be taken. Inside a short space of time, the coach should ensure that a large number of free kicks are taken from a wide variety of positions, including positions inside the penalty area for indirect free kicks.

Key factors

1 Observe that an outfield player always sets the wall in position.

2 Observe that the correct number of players are placed in the wall and that they:

   a Prevent the bent shot round the outside of the wall.

   b Are sized correctly – tallest on the outside, shortest on the inside.

   c Protect themselves correctly.

3   Observe the position of the goalkeeper in relation to the wall.

4   Observe that the kick is always threatened from the inside
    position.

5   Observe that the players seal off the vital spaces.

6   Observe that the players outside the wall know when to adjust
    their position to mark opponents and when to retain their
    position in space.

7   Observe that the players know how to defend against indirect
    free kicks in the penalty area.

Corner kicks

Defending at corner kicks involves exactly the same principles as defending at free kicks. You could organize a player to threaten the kick and to disturb the kicker.

The position that the defending player adopts will depend on whether the attacking player takes an inswing or an outswing kick. If the kick is an outswinger, then they will position near to the goal line – in position A in Figure 61. If the kick is an inswinger, they will position further out from the goal line in position B.

Figure 61

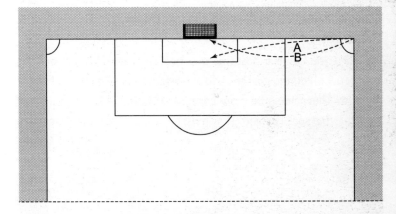

The technique of threatening the kick is to position 1 yard (0.9 m) inside the anticipated line of flight and move into the line as the kicker is approaching the ball. The late movement of the defending player may cause the kicker to look at the defender instead of the ball, or change their mind about the line of the kick. If the kicker does either of the above, it will adversely affect their technique.

The opponents may decide to play the ball short. Should this happen, the defending player is in a position to try to prevent the opposition moving nearer to the goal. They are also in a position to delay the cross into the goalmouth. It should, however, be understood that if the opposition does take a short corner, a two vs. one situation in the attackers' favour is not satisfactory from the defensive point of view.

The position of the goalkeeper

The position of the goalkeeper is critical. The major threat to the goal from corners is caused by the inswing kick directed towards the front half of the goal. Attacking teams will not only use the inswing technique frequently, but they will also support that play by placing several players in the area of the near post, one or more of whom are likely to be on the goal line.

The position of the players on the posts

The near post

The player on the near post (the post nearest to the kicker) should be 1 yard (0.9 m) off the goal line and at least 1 yard (0.9 metre) in front of the post. They should be more concerned about the space in front of them than the space behind. They must be prepared to seal off the space

Figure 62

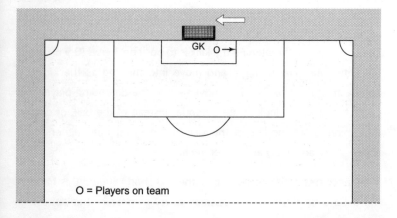

O = Players on team

near to the goal line and in front of the near post. Should the goalkeeper come out from goal to take a high cross, then he/she should tuck in, on the goal line, inside the post to defend the goal. They will certainly have time to achieve that objective.

The far post

Most goalkeepers feel more comfortable when they position halfway across their goal, if the player defending the far post is in a position along the goal line, inside the far post (Figure 63).

Figure 63

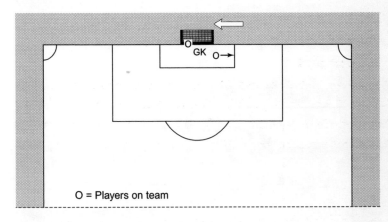

O = Players on team

Defending the near-post area

Figure 64 shows the positions of the two players in question, O5 and O4, O4 should position 2 yards (1.8 m) inside the 6-yard (5.5-m) area. Their concern must be the space in front of them and the space between them and O3. The foot position of O4 is very important and should be that of a sprint start. This will enable O4 to move quickly into the space in front of him/her. O5 will be 1 yard (0.9 m) inside the 6-yard (5.5-m) area and in the front half of the goal.

Figure 64

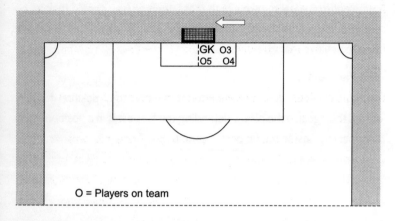

O = Players on team

Figure 65

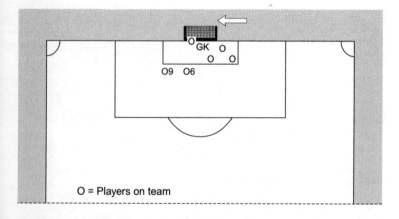

O = Players on team

Defending the far-post area

While the near-post area is the most vulnerable, it must not be assumed that goals cannot, or will not, be scored in the area of the far post.

In Figure 65, O6 is positioned in the back half of the goal and 1 yard (0.9 m) outside the 6-yard (5.5-m) area. Likewise, O9 is positioned at the back of the 6-yard (5.5-m) area and 1 yard (0.9 m) outside the area. Both O6 and O9 are in positions to make aerial challenges for the ball in the far-post area. Both of them must position in a manner which gives them the chance to observe movements in the back half of the penalty area.

Defending the area between the 6-yard (5.5-m) and the 18-yard (16.5-m) lines

As the ball goes out from the goal area, so the danger lessens. There is the possibility, nevertheless, that the ball may be played directly into the area between the 6-yard (5.5-m) line and the 18-yard (16.5-m) line, or that the ball may be partially cleared into that area. The final three players should, therefore, be deployed in that area (Figure 66).

Figure 66

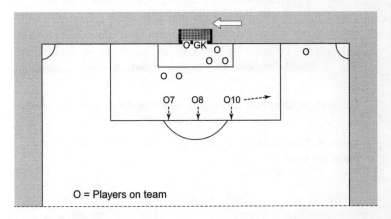

O7, O8 and O10 are positioned just beyond the penalty spot as shown in Figure 66. These are rough guidelines because the positions of opponents may cause one or more of them to adjust their positions. Their main task is to prevent a strike at goal from the edge of the penalty area.

O10, however, has an additional task: he/she must watch the situation in the area of the kicker. If the opposition introduces a second attacker into that area, thereby creating a two vs. one situation for a short corner, then O10 must move out to the corner to equalize the numbers. Should that happen, then O7 and O8 must adjust their positions.

Once the ball has been cleared by the defence, the whole defence should move up and out of the penalty area as quickly as possible in order to support the ball and play as many opponents as possible offside.

Key factors

1 Observe the technique of the player threatening the kick.

2 Observe the position of the goalkeeper.

3 Observe the position of the players in the near-post area, and how they attack the ball.

4 Observe the position of the players in the far-post area, and how they deal with balls played into their area.

5 Observe the position of the players between the 6-yard (5.5-m) line and the 18-yard (16.5-m) line, and how they deal with balls played directly into that area and balls partially cleared into that area.

6 Observe the reaction and adjustments of the players to a short corner.

7 Observe how quickly the players move out of the penalty area once the ball is cleared.

Except for the unlikely source of a direct goal from the corner kick, goals from corners will require attackers to connect with the corner. Establish simple rules to avoid goals from being conceded: be first to the ball; attack the ball; aim for height and distance; try to avoid the ball going to ground in your penalty area; pressure and block secondary scoring opportunities.

Defending at corners. Zonal or player-for-player marking?

Most coaches will agree to incorporate some zonal marking at corners. They will invariably have a player free from player for player marking duties to defend the area in front of the near post and may have one player on each of the posts. Players on the edge of the penalty area will defend this 'area' rather than mark players. The major question revolves around whether your team 'marks' the three or four major headers of the opposition or defends the key spaces from which headed strikes will be attempted.

Best Practice **Zonal** marking allows you to place your team's most appropriate players where you want them – not where the opponents decide to move them to. Regardless of the opposition everyone knows their job, week in, week out. **Player for player** marking can allow you to match up your best defensive headers against the opponent's best, but your best defensive players can be dragged out of position. Both systems require players who can attack the ball with conviction and be first to the ball – without these qualities no system will prove successful.

'Zonal marking' becomes 'player-for-player marking' when an opponent wants to attack your zone.

Throw-ins

Throw-ins occur more frequently than any other type of set play. Some players regard them merely as a way of restarting the game, unaware of how often goals are scored from moves begun with a throw. Because of this, many players lose concentration at throws and leave opponents unmarked.

Defending against throw-ins is usually a matter of applying the basic principles of defending. Special tactical arrangements such as those at free kicks and corners are usually neither practical nor necessary. The only exception to this rule is when the opposition is set up for a long throw in their attacking third. At ordinary throw-ins, however, defenders need to do three things.

1   Defenders should take up positions in goal side where they can watch both their immediate opponent and the ball.

2   Defenders tend to mark too closely at throw-ins. This mistake can be costly, for the attacker can create space for themselves with a quick change of direction. At a throw-in, attackers usually stand around 15–20 yards (14–18 m) from the thrower. If this is the case, the defender should stand 2–3 yards (1.8–2.8 m) goal side of the player they are marking. At that distance they can cover any quick move by their opponent and also make up ground to challenge should the ball be thrown to their attacker.

3   Defenders should put the player receiving the ball under heavy pressure, making control and one-touch play more difficult for them. The receiver has to pass or control a dropping ball, a particularly difficult task under pressure.

Long throws

The long throw, rarely seen 30 years ago, has become a major set piece in modern football and a useful source of goals. Players' throwing techniques have improved. Not only can many players throw the ball long distances, they can do so with a relatively low, flat trajectory, flinging the ball at speed into the mid-goal area. Defending against such a throw is no easy task.

The one thing attackers do not have on their side is surprise. Everyone can see when a long throw is coming. Defenders should go into pre-set positions, chosen with regard to the following factors:

• The player taking the throw should be marked by a defender standing 2–3 yards (1.8–2.8 m) away in a line between the thrower and the goal. The defender's job is to try to force the thrower to steepen the trajectory of the throw. The higher the trajectory, the longer the ball is in the air. Time, as ever, works in favour of the defence.

- The player positioned to receive the throw should be marked from behind, but not too closely. The defender must have the space in which to move forward and attack the ball.

- Someone should mark the space in front of the player receiving the throw (O2 in Figure 67). The ideal position is 2–3 yards (1.8–2.8 m) in front of them. Placing a defender here not only puts pressure on the receiver, but also the thrower.

- The goalkeeper should stand in the near half of the goal. It is rarely possible for them to make a realistic challenge for the ball from the far half of the goal.

- As much space as possible should be sealed off in the penalty area. The attacking team will push several players forward to support the long throw, ranging them across the width of the penalty area to challenge for partial clearances or flick-ons. One player will be detailed to attack the far-post area. All these players must be denied space.

Figure 67

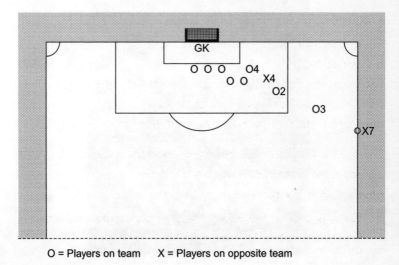

O = Players on team   X = Players on opposite team

Figure 67 shows a typical defensive arrangement against a long throw. Nine outfield players have been brought back to meet the threat. Apart from O2, O3 and O4, all the others are marking space. All the spaces in the penalty area must be marked. Although defenders can make slight adjustments to mark an attacker in their space, they should not leave the area which they are responsible for marking in order to mark a player. Their job is to deal with secondary shooting opportunities. Wherever the ball lands, a defensive player should be on hand to immediately challenge for it, to clear it or at least block the shot. It is unlikely that the attacking team will put more than seven players in the penalty area, and the number and position of the defending players shown here should be enough to deal with seven attackers.

Summary

- You can use the defending at set plays as an important platform for all your team's defending.

- The defending of free kicks, corner kicks and throw-ins can provide suitable starting positions in an 11 vs. 11 coaching situation for you to coach on a number of defensive aspects.

- Success at defending set plays will improve the overall team's confidence to defend effectively. Nothing erodes a team's morale more than to defend periodically through a game only to lose a goal at a set play.

- It is important that the players understand the respective roles and it will be of value to involve them in decision making to establish the overall team 'rules' for defending at set plays.

Self testers

1 Give three reasons why set plays are difficult to defend against.

2 What three qualities are needed for successful defending at set plays?

3 Give an example of where you would coach your team to cover the danger areas when defending a corner.

Action plan

What is your preference for defending free kicks and corners?

How do you like to organize your players to gain maximum

advantage? What is your reasoning for this? Once you have
clarified your own thinking for set plays, how would you defend
against your own team's set plays? Imagine you are an opposition
scout who has watched your team defend at set plays. What do
you believe to be your team's strengths and weaknesses when
defending set plays?

Conclusion

This book has highlighted some of the aspects involved in coaching teams. There are, of course, other aspects to consider including talent identification, team selection, team building, leadership, and how and what to coach with regard to individual players, team units and the whole team itself. However, we hope that this book has provided sound guidance and advice on how to develop your coaching skills.

To further improve your ability to coach players and teams you are strongly recommended to undertake one of the FA Coaching courses.

In conjunction with completing a coaching course, it is important that you practise coaching, and practise planning and evaluating your coaching sessions. Try to spend the same amount of time on evaluating your coaching as you do on planning. Evaluate yourself, get a friend to evaluate you, and attempt to gauge the reactions of players. What works? What doesn't work?

The overall aim of this book is to spur the reader to be a life-long student of the game. We hope that you continue to be receptive to new ideas and that you satisfy your thirst for knowledge.

The FA

LEARNING

Contacts

Fédération Internationale de Football Association (FIFA)
FIFA House
Hitzigweg 11
PO Box 85
8030 Zurich
Switzerland
Tel: +41-43/222 7777
Fax: +41-43/222 7878
Internet: http://www.fifa.com

Confederations

Asian Football Confederation (AFC)
AFC House, Jalan 1/155B
Bukit Jalil
Kuala Lumpur 57000
Malaysia
Tel: +60-3/8994 3388
Fax: +60-3/8994 2689
Internet: http://www.footballasia.com

Confédération Africaine de Football (CAF)
3 Abdel Khalek Sarwat Street
El Hay El Motamayez
PO Box 23
6th October City
Egypt
Tel: +20-2/837 1000
Fax: +20-2/837 0006
Internet: http://www.cafonline.com

Confederation of North, Central American and Caribbean Association Football (CONCACAF)
Central American and Caribbean Association Football
725 Fifth Avenue, 17th Floor
New York, NY 10022
USA
Tel: +1-212/308 0044
Fax: +1-212/308 1851
Internet: http://www.concacaf.net

Confederación Sudamericana de Fútbol (CONMEBOL)
Autopista Aeropuerto Internacional y
Leonismo Luqueño
Luque (Gran Asunción)
Paraguay
Tel: +595-21/645 781
Fax: +595-21/645 791
Internet: http://www.conmebol.com

Oceania Football Confederation (OFC)
Ericsson Stadium
12 Maurice Road
PO Box 62 586
Penrose
Auckland
New Zealand
Tel: +64-9/525 8161
Fax: +64-9/525 8164
Internet: http://www.oceaniafootball
    .com

Union European Football Association (UEFA)
Route de Genève 46
Nyon 1260
Switzerland
Tel: +41-22/994 4444
Fax: +41-22/994 4488
Internet: http://www.uefa.com

Associations

Argentina
Asociación del Fútbol Argentino (AFA)
Viamonte 1366/76
Buenos Aires 1053
Tel: ++54-11/4372 7900
Fax: ++54-11/4375 4410
Internet: http://www.afa.org.ar

Australia
Soccer Australia Limited (ASF)
Level 3
East Stand, Stadium Australia
Edwin Flack Avenue
Homebush NSW 2127
Tel: ++61-2/9739 5555
Fax: ++61-2/9739 5590
Internet: http://www.socceraustralia
    .com.au

Belgium
Union Royale Belge des Sociétés de Football Assocation (URBSFA/KBV)
145 Avenue Houba de Strooper
Bruxelles 1020
Tel: ++32-2/477 1211
Fax: ++32-2/478 2391
Internet: http://www.footbel.com

Brazil
Confederação Brasileira de Futebol (CBF)
Rua Victor Civita 66
Bloco 1 – Edificio 5 – 5 Andar
Barra da Tijuca
Rio de Janeiro 22775-040
Tel: ++55-21/3870 3610
Fax: ++55-21/3870 3612
Internet: http://www.cbfnews.com

Cameroon
Fédération Camerounaise de Football (FECAFOOT)
Case postale 1116
Yaoundé
Tel: ++237/221 0012
Fax: ++237/221 6662
Internet: http://www.cameroon.fifa.com

Canada
The Canadian Soccer Association (CSA)
Place Soccer Canada
237 Metcalfe Street
Ottawa ONT K2P 1R2
Tel: ++1-613/237 7678
Fax: ++1-613/237 1516
Internet: http://www.canadasoccer.com

Costa Rica
Federación Costarricense de Fútbol (FEDEFUTBOL)
Costado Norte Estatua León Cortés
San José 670-1000
Tel: ++506/222 1544
Fax: ++506/255 2674
Internet: http://www.fedefutbol.com

Croatia
Croatian Football Federation (HNS)
Rusanova 13
Zagreb 10 000
Tel: ++385-1/236 1555
Fax: ++385-1/244 1501
Internet: http://www.hns-cff.hr

Czech Republic
Football Association of Czech Republic (CMFS)
Diskarska 100
Praha 6 16017
Tel: ++420-2/3302 9111
Fax: ++420-2/3335 3107
Internet: http://www.fotbal.cz

Denmark
Danish Football Association (DBU)
Idrættens Hus
Brøndby Stadion 20
Brøndby 2605
Tel: ++45-43/262 222
Fax: ++45-43/262 245
Internet: http://www.dbu.dk

England
The Football Association (The FA)
25 Soho Square
London W1D 4FA
Tel: ++44-207/745 4545
Fax: ++44-207/745 4546
Internet: http://www.TheFA.com

Finland
Suomen Palloliitto (SPL/FBF)
Urheilukatu 5
PO Box 191
Helsinki 00251
Tel: ++358-9/7421 51
Fax: ++358-9/7421 5200
Internet: http://www.palloliitto.fi

France
Fédération Française de Football (FFF)
60 Bis Avenue d'Iéna
Paris 75116
Tel: ++33-1/4431 7300
Fax: ++33-1/4720 8296
Internet: http://www.fff.fr

Germany
Deutscher Fussball-Bund (DFB)
Otto-Fleck-Schneise 6
Postfach 71 02 65
Frankfurt Am Main 60492
Tel: ++49-69/678 80
Fax: ++49-69/678 8266
Internet: http://www.dfb.de

Greece
Hellenic Football Federation (HFF)
137 Singrou Avenue
Nea Smirni
Athens 17121
Tel: ++30-210/930 6000
Fax: ++30-210/935 9666
Internet: http://www.epo.gr

Ireland Republic
The Football Association of Ireland (FAI)
80 Merrion Square, South
Dublin 2
Tel: ++353-1/676 6864
Fax: ++353-1/661 0931
Internet: http://www.fai.ie

Italy
Federazione Italiana Giuoco Calcio (FIGC)
Via Gregorio Allegri, 14
Roma 00198
Tel: ++39-06/84 911
Fax: ++39-06/84 912 526
Internet: http://www.figc.it

Japan
Japan Football Association (JFA)
JFA House
3-10-15, Hongo
Bunkyo-ku
Tokyo 113-0033
Tel: ++81-3/3830 2004
Fax: ++81-3/3830 2005
Internet: http://www.jfa.or.jp

Kenya
Kenya Football Federation (KFF)
PO Box 40234
Nairobi
Tel: ++254-2/608 422
Fax: ++254-2/249 855
Email: kff@todays.co.ke

Korea Republic
Korea Football Association (KFA)
1-131 Sinmunno, 2-ga
Jongno-Gu
Seoul 110-062
Tel: ++82-2/733 6764
Fax: ++82-2/735 2755
Internet: http://www.kfa.or.kr

Mexico
Federación Mexicana de Fútbol Asociación, A.C. (FMF)
Colima No. 373
Colonia Roma
Mexico, D.F. 06700
Tel: ++52-55/5241 0190
Fax: ++52-55/5241 0191
Internet: http://www.femexfut.org.mx

Netherlands
Koninklijke Nederlandse Voetbalbond (KNVB)
Woudenbergseweg 56–58
PO Box 515
Am Zeist 3700 AM
Tel: ++31-343/499 201
Fax: ++31-343/499 189
Internet: http://www.knvb.nl

Nigeria
Nigeria Football Association (NFA)
Plot 2033, Olusegun
Obasanjo Way, Zone 7, Wuse Abuja
PO Box 5101 Garki
Abuja
Tel: ++234-9/523 7326
Fax: ++234-9/523 7327
Email: nfa@microaccess.com

Northern Ireland
Irish Football Association Ltd.
(IFA)
20 Windsor Avenue
Belfast BT9 6EE
Tel: ++44-28/9066 9458
Fax: ++44-28/9066 7620
Internet: http://www.irishfa.com

Paraguay
Asociación Paraguaya de Fútbol
(APF)
Estadio de los Defensores del Chaco
Calle Mayor Martinez 1393
Asunción
Tel: ++595-21/480 120
Fax: ++595-21/480 124
Internet: http://www.apf.org.py

Poland
Polish Football Association (PZPN)
Polski Zwiazek Pilki Noznej
Miodowa 1
Warsaw 00-080
Tel: ++48-22/827 0914
Fax: ++48-22/827 0704
Internet: http://www.pzpn.pl

Portugal
Federação Portuguesa de Futebol
(FPF)
Praça de Alegria, N. 25
PO Box 21.100
Lisbon 1250-004
Tel: ++351-21/325 2700
Fax: ++351-21/325 2780
Internet: http://www.fpf.pt

Romania
Romanian Football Federation
(FRF)
House of Football
Str. Serg. Serbanica Vasile 12
Bucharest 73412
Tel: ++40-21/325 0678
Fax: ++40-21/325 0679
Internet: http://www.frf.ro

Russia
Football Union of Russia (RFU)
8 Luzhnetskaya Naberezhnaja
Moscow 119 992
Tel: ++7-095/201 1637
Fax: ++7-502/220 2037
Internet: http://www.rfs.ru

Scotland
The Scottish Football Association
(SFA)
Hampden Park
Glasgow G42 9AY
Tel: ++44-141/616 6000
Fax: ++44-141/616 6001
Internet: http://www.scottishfa.co.uk

South Africa
South African Football
Association (SAFA)
First National Bank Stadium
PO Box 910
Johannesburg 2000
Tel: ++27-11/494 3522
Fax: ++27-11/494 3013
Internet: http://www.safa.net

Spain
Real Federación Española de Fútbol (RFEF)
Ramon y Cajal, s/n
Apartado postale 385
Madrid 28230
Tel: ++34-91/495 9800
Fax: ++34-91/495 9801
Internet: http://www.rfef.es

Sweden
Svenska Fotbollförbundet (SVFF)
PO Box 1216
Solna 17 123
Tel: ++46-8/735 0900
Fax: ++46-8/735 0901
Internet: http://www.svenskfotboll.se

Switzerland
Schweizerischer Fussball-Verband (SFV/ASF)
Postfach
Bern 15 3000
Tel: ++41-31/950 8111
Fax: ++41-31/950 8181
Internet: http://www.football.ch

Tunisia
Fédération Tunisienne de Football (FTF)
Maison des Fédérations Sportives
Cité Olympique
Tunis 1003
Tel: ++216-71/233 303
Fax: ++216-71/767 929
Internet: http://www.ftf.org.tn

Turkey
Türkiye Futbol Federasyonu (TFF)
Konaklar Mah. Ihlamurlu Sok. 9
4. Levent
Istanbul 80620
Tel: ++90-212/282 7020
Fax: ++90-212/282 7015
Internet: http://www.tff.org

United States of America
US Soccer Federation (USSF)
US Soccer House
1801 S. Prairie Avenue
Chicago IL 60616
Tel: ++1-312/808 1300
Fax: ++1-312/808 1301
Internet: http://www.ussoccer.com

Uruguay
Asociación Uruguaya de Fútbol (AUF)
Guayabo 1531
Montevideo 11200
Tel: ++59-82/400 4814
Fax: ++59-82/409 0550
Internet: http://www.auf.org.uy

Wales
The Football Association of Wales, Ltd (FAW)
Plymouth Chambers
3 Westgate Street
Cardiff CF10 1DP
Tel: ++44-29/2037 2325
Fax: ++44-29/2034 3961
Internet: http://www.faw.org.uk

For details of County FAs please see **www.TheFA.com**/Grassroots

LEARNING

Index

All about FA Learning

FA Learning is the Educational Division of The FA and is responsible for the delivery, co-ordination and promotion of its extensive range of educational products and services. This includes all courses and resources for coaching, refereeing, psychology, sports science, medical exercise, child protection, crowd safety and teacher training.

The diverse interests of those involved in football ensures that FA Learning remains committed to providing resources and activities suitable for all individuals whatever their interests, experience or level of expertise.

Whether you're a Premier League Manager, sports psychologist or interested parent, our aim is to have courses and resources available that will improve your knowledge and understanding.

If you've enjoyed reading this book and found the content useful then why not take a look at FA Learning's website to find out the types of courses and additional resources available to help you continue your football development.

The website contains information on all the national courses and events managed by The FA as well as information on a number of online resources:

- **Psychology for Soccer Level 1 – Our first online qualification.**
- **Soccer Star – Free online coaching tool for young players.**
- **Soccer Parent – Free online course for parents.**

All these resources can be accessed at home from your own PC and are currently used by thousands of people across the world.

Psychology for Soccer Level 1

Enrol today and join hundreds of others around the world taking part in FA Learning's first ever online qualification.

This pioneering project is the first of its kind to be provided by any Football Governing Body and is available to anyone with access to the internet. There are no additional qualifications required to take part other than an interest in learning more about the needs of young players and an email address!

The course is aimed at coaches, parents and teachers of 7–12 year olds looking to gain an introduction to psychology and features modules based on 'true to life' player, coach and parent scenarios.

Psychology for Soccer Level 1 is a completely interactive, multimedia learning experience. Don't just take our word for it, read some of the comments from those that have already completed the course:

'Wow what a wonderful course! Thank you for the time and effort to make this possible.' **Tracy Scott**

'Just passed the final assessment … it was a good experience to learn this way and hopefully more qualifications will become available in this format. Thanks.' **Shayne Hall**

'I am a professional football coach working in schools and clubs and have travelled all around the world. I have really enjoyed the literature in this course and it has made me think about how I should address my coaching sessions. I want to progress in the field of sport psychology and this course has whetted my appetite for this subject.' **Chris Rafael Sabater**

The course modules are:

- Psychology and Soccer
- Motivation
- Learning and Acquiring skills
- Psychological Development
- Environment and Social Influences

In addition to the five course modules, learners also have access to a number of further benefits included as part of the course fee. The benefits include:

- **Three months support from qualified FA tutors**
- **Classroom specific online discussion forums**
- **A global online discussion forum**
- **All successful students receive a FA Qualification in psychology**

- **An exclusive resource area containing over 100 articles and web links relating to coaching 7–12 year olds.**

Within the five modules, there are over 20 sessions totaling over eight hours worth of content. Including the use of discussion forums, resource area and the course tasks, we anticipate the course will take on average 20 hours to complete.

For more information and to enroll on the course visit
www.**TheFA.com**/FALearning.

THE OFFICIAL FA GUIDE TO
FITNESS FOR FOOTBALL

Be a part of the game

The Official FA Guide to Fitness for Football provides essential knowledge and advice for everyone who plays the game.

This book includes:
- **basic physiology and nutrition**
- **training strategies**
- **the physiological differences between adults and children.**

Packed with practical exercises, information and expert advice, this book will improve your understanding and enhance your ability and enjoyment of the world's greatest game.

The author, **Dr Richard Hawkins**, is the Deputy Head of Exercise Science at The Football Association.

FA Learning
'learning through football'

TheFA.com/FALearning

Visit the website for information on all FA Learning's educational activities.

LEARNING

THE OFFICIAL FA GUIDE TO
RUNNING A CLUB

Be a part of the game

The Official FA Guide to Running a Club is written for anyone
involved in the administration side of the game.

This book includes:
- **advice on how to start and run a club**
- **who to turn to for help**
- **how to deal with any problems that may occur**
- **finance, administration, PR and marketing.**

Packed with practical exercises, information and expert advice,
this book will improve your understanding and enhance your
ability and enjoyment of the world's greatest game.

The author, **Les Howie**, is responsible for the development of all
clubs in the non-professional national game for The Football
Association

FA Learning
'learning through football'

TheFA.com/FALearning

Visit the website for information on all FA
Learning's educational activities.

THE OFFICIAL FA GUIDE TO
PSYCHOLOGY FOR FOOTBALL

Be a part of the game

The Official FA Guide to Psychology for Football is an introductory guide for anyone who wants to understand the needs of young players.

This book includes:
- **understanding the motivation, learning and development of players**
- **the affect of a player's environment**
- **how to develop individual strategies.**

Packed with practical exercises, information and expert advice, this book will improve your understanding and enhance your ability and enjoyment of the world's greatest game.

The author, **Dr Andy Cale**, is The Football Association's Education Advisor and was previously a lecturer in Sports Psychology at Loughborough University.

FA Learning
'learning through football'

TheFA.com/FALearning

Visit the website for information on all FA Learning's educational activities.

LEARNING

THE OFFICIAL FA GUIDE TO
BASIC REFEREEING

Be a part of the game

The Official FA Guide to Basic Refereeing is essential reading for all referees and those in training, and also provides vital knowledge for anyone involved in the game.

This book includes:
- **the laws of the game and how to apply them**
- **recognising free kick and offside offences**
- **important advice about managing players.**

Packed with practical exercises, information and expert advice, this book will improve your understanding and enhance your ability and enjoyment of the world's greatest game.

The author, **John Baker**, is Head of Refereeing at The Football Association, responsible for the 30,000 registered referees in England.

FA Learning
'learning through football'

TheFA.com/FALearning

Visit the website for information on all FA Learning's educational activities.

THE OFFICIAL FA GUIDE FOR
FOOTBALL PARENTS

Be a part of the game

The Official FA Guide for Football Parents is essential reading for any parent of a young footballer, who wants to get involved and help their child to do their very best.

This book includes:
- **choosing a club and being involved in it**
- **sharing the football interest**
- **being a 'garden coach'.**

Packed with practical exercises, information and expert advice, this book will improve your understanding and enhance your ability and enjoyment of the world's greatest game.

The author, **Les Howie**, is responsible for the development of all clubs in the non-professional national game for The Football Association.

FA Learning
'learning through football'

TheFA.com/FALearning

Visit the website for information on all FA
Learning's educational activities.

LEARNING